易学学中文

Easy Chinese

Basic Text and Workbook

Accompanied by the
Easy Chinese Tutor CD-ROM

Mandarin

Level I

Edward C. Chang

EMNES
SYSTEMS

Gaithersburg, Maryland

Emnes Systems
Gaithersburg, Maryland
www.emnes.com

First Edition
Easy Chinese: Mandarin Level I
Copyright © 2003 by Edward C. Chang

Library of Congress Control Number: 2003107180

ISBN 0-9661636-3-X

Cover Design by Emily Wang
Original Cover Photo by Mimi Chang

Printed in the United States of America.

Contents

日 rì	月 yuè	山 shān	川 chuān	木 mù
土 tǔ	水 shuǐ	火 huǒ	上 shàng	下 xià
大 dà	小 xiǎo			

明 míng	林 lín	森 sēn	炎 yán	晶 jīng
尖 jiān	人 rén	口 kǒu	子 zǐ	女 nǚ
田 tián	目 mù	好 hǎo	心 xīn	

中 zhōng	外 wài	牛 niú	馬 mǎ	也 yě
門 mén	天 tiān	地 dì	有 yǒu	沒 méi
是 shì	不 bù	夫 fū	婦 fù	家 jiā
雨 yǔ				

一 yī	二 èr	三 sān	四 sì	五 wǔ
六 liù	七 qī	八 bā	九 jiǔ	十 shí
你 nǐ	您 nín	他 tā	我 wǒ	們 men
她 tā	它 tā	的 de	了 le	去 qù
出 chū				

Easy Chinese Tutor CD-ROM

Preface

This book serves both as a manual to accompany the *Easy Chinese Tutor* software and as a basic text and workbook for the *Easy Chinese* Self-Study Course. Although the book and software overlap in content, they each offer different illustrative sentences and exercises. Together they should give you, the learner, plenty of opportunity to discover the fundamentals of the Chinese language.

One of the most important issues in the development of a tutorial program in Chinese is this: Which form of Chinese characters—traditional or simplified—should be learned or taught? Most Chinese language programs today, whether in the form of book or software, usually adhere to only one form while excluding the other. The choice of character form to be included in a book or software is often based on ideological, geographical, or practical considerations. For example, it is impractical, if not impossible, to include both character forms in one book— it would be quite cumbersome and very confusing. Moreover, it would place even more demand, in time and effort, on the learner to learn a language that is already considered to be one of the most difficult in the world.

In this program, I attempt to help you develop, with just a little extra effort, the skill and ability required to read both traditional and simplified characters. I believe that it is rewarding as well as practical for you to be able to read both forms in today's world of Internet connectivity and instant written communication. Although you will be shown both types of characters in both the software and the book, it is really up to you to decide the character form with which you write your Chinese.

I certainly underestimated the time and effort required to complete this project. It is my sincere hope that this program will significantly help reduce your learning time and minimize whatever frustration you may have in the learning process. Every effort has been made to accommodate learners of different backgrounds by creating a comprehensive tutorial program. As a result, you may encounter some information that you already know, in which case, you may consider this information as a basic review. It is my assumption that any individual, regardless of his or her background characteristics, can successsfully complete this course at his or her own pace.

A project of this magnitude could not be completed without the help of several people. I want to thank those who have offered me suggestions, encouragement, and support. I especially want to thank Allen Zhang, Fu Shan Nie, Lun Cheung Ku, Mimi Chang, and Emily Wang for their valuable contributions and assistance at various stages of this project development.

Edward C. Chang

Frequently Asked Questions

About the Course

What do you mean by "*Easy Chinese?*"

The term "*Easy Chinese*," as used in this course, refers collectively to: (1) a group of Chinese characters, about 800 in number, that appear most often in modern Chinese publications and everyday correspondence; (2) the step-by-step approach in presenting these characters in the form of compound words, phrases, and sentences; (3) the system, methodology, and tools that are used in organizing these Chinese characters into a predetermined learning sequence; and (4) the basic text of this course.

What are the major components of the *Easy Chinese* course?

The course consists of the basic text, workbook, and the *Easy Chinese Tutor* (CD-ROM).

How often will I see these *Easy Chinese* characters in a typical Chinese publication?

As an estimate, more than 80 percent of the characters found in modern Chinese publications come from these 800 or so characters.

For whom is your course most appropriate?

Easy Chinese is designed for anyone who wants to learn the Chinese language on his or her own with the help of a computer.

Can I use this program to supplement regular classroom instruction?

Absolutely. As a tutorial program, *Easy Chinese* can be flexibly used to supplement regular instruction.

In what fundamental ways, in terms of instructional approach, does your program differ from other programs?

First, you will learn Chinese one step at a time. Each step will be small, gradual, and manageable. You will never be overwhelmed by the amount of material you need to learn at any given time. In fact, each step consists of no more than three new characters.

Second, learning is very precise. You will know exactly what to expect and what you will need

1

to accomplish. Since the program is self-paced, you can learn at the pace that is most comfortable for you. Take as much time as you want to thoroughly learn the material provided in any given step.

Third, learning is highly structured and systematic. By design, each Chinese character in the learning sequence has a special role to play in developing and expanding your language network. Thus, you will not learn characters in isolation; you will learn them as necessary components in the formation of a network of links, connections, and associations. Typically, the more links you have in your language network, the more efficient you will become in learning the Chinese language.

Is your program designed for beginners?

The first course assumes that you have no prior background in the Chinese language and is designed for people who have never studied the Chinese language before.

Which type of characters do you teach: simplified or traditional?

Both. With just a little extra effort, you can learn both types simultaneously. Actually, most characters in the first course are the same in both the simplified and traditional forms.

I want to be able to recognize both types of Chinese characters. However, I only want to learn to write Chinese in the simplified form. Can I do that?

Absolutely. *Easy Chinese* allows you the flexibility to choose the character form that best meets your needs.

Are the terms "Chinese character" and "Chinese word" synonymous?

Not exactly. While a single Chinese character by itself may function as a word, a Chinese word often consists of two or more characters.

How many characters and words can I learn in the first course?

There are only 136 characters in the first course. However, the combinations of these same characters can form more than 700 compound words and phrases. Thus, the total number of words you can expect to learn in the first course is more than 700.

How many sentences are included in the first course?

From the 136 characters and words that are introduced to you in the first course, you will see how to construct more than 1,000 sentences.

About the *Easy Chinese Tutor* CD-ROM

What is the *Easy Chinese Tutor?*

The *Easy Chinese Tutor* is a computer-based program designed to help its users master the contents of *Easy Chinese* one step at a time. The tutor is brought to you in the form of a CD-ROM.

What are the major components of each lesson?

The two major components in each lesson are text and exercises. In addition, learning tools such as phonetic drills, tests, and a copybook facilitate the learning process.

How is the text component in each lesson organized?

The material in the text component is organized into a series of steps. Each step normally consists of two new characters, compound words, phrases, and a sentence block. Each new step is built upon the information acquired in previous steps. Any component in a given step is also divided into sub-components. For example, by clicking on a character on a virtual page, you will immediately see a character menu that offers the following learning feature options: stroke order, writing style, pronunciation, character combinations, and association.

How will I learn to *write* a character?

Two methods are used in this program to teach character strokes. When you click on the "stroke" button, you will be asked to select one of the two ways of displaying the strokes. By clicking on the "**continuous**" button, the strokes will appear as though someone is actually writing the character. By clicking on the "**discontinuous**" button, the strokes will move, one by one, from a starting position to the next location where the next stroke is to be placed. A "**simplified**" button will appear if a character has a simplified form.

How can I practice my character writing?

You can print a sheet of "hollow" characters and use it as a template for writing characters. To print these sheets, open a graphic program that is available in your computer and find the "copybk" directory in your *Easy Chinese Tutor* (CD-ROM). Open the appropriate lesson (i.e. "less1", " less5") in which the character (represented by its pronunciation) is located. Finally, click "print."

What can I learn by using the character "combination" tool?

You can substantially increase your Chinese vocabulary by combining the new character with those you have already learned. When you click on the "**combination**" button on the character menu, you will see a screen with a large circle surrounded by several small circles. You will see that within each small circle is a character you have already learned. When you click on a character within a small circle, it will move to the center of the large circle and line up to form a word or phrase with the new character. As the character moves, you will hear the voice of a native speaker saying the word or phrase. At the same time, you will see the meaning of the combination and its phonetic transcription.

How can the "association" feature help me?

The "association" feature serves two purposes. One is to acquaint you with the origin of the character; the other is to help you remember the meanings of the character by thinking about the visual imagery created by each statement. This feature is intended mainly as a mnemonic device (a memory aid), and should not be used as a scholarly interpretation of the character's origin.

With what tools can I learn the illustrative sentences?

As you click on each sentence block that appears on the virtual page, you will see a menu that consists of the following buttons: **explain, expand, pinyin, simplified, and examples**. Each tool provides a unique way for you to learn some aspects of a sentence.

What can I learn by using the "explain" feature?

With the "explain" feature, you will be able to develop a clear understanding of the meaning and syntax of the illustrative sentences. When you click on a particular sentence, several boxes will appear on the screen. Inside each box is a word or word group. The function of the word(s) in the sentence can be easily identified by the position of the box and by the color of the words. For example, the order of the boxes usually corresponds to the subject, verb, and object of the sentence. When you click or press a key to continue, the meaning corresponding to each sentence element will also appear. A click with the mouse will produce an English translation of the entire sentence. This feature is designed to help you develop an insight about the sentence structure without being overwhelmed by the grammatical details.

Are there discussions about grammar anywhere in the program?

A "grammar" button sometimes appears on the screen of the illustrative sentences to provide information about Chinese grammar.

What can I do with the "expand" feature?

The "expand" feature shows how to expand the lesson by substituting various sentence elements. At least nine possible combinations will show how you can create sentences with different meanings.

How can I use the "example" feature?

When you click on the "example" button, you will see four sentences written in English. You will be asked to translate these sentences into Chinese by utilizing new and previously learned characters. If you click on each English sentence, the appropriate Chinese characters for composing that sentence will show up on the screen.

Can I learn to *say* the sentences that appear on the virtual page?

By clicking on the "pinyin" button, you will hear pronunciations of the sentences that appear on the virtual page by a native speaker. You can practice speaking by listening and by repeating these sentences.

Can I see the same sentences written in simplified form?

With the "simplified" feature, you can switch back and forth between the simplified or traditional versions by clicking on the "switch" button.

Exercises

What types of exercises can I do in each lesson?

Five different types of exercises are provided in each lesson: character drills, stroke orders, pronunciation, phrases and sentences, and listening. You will access the exercise menu by clicking on the "exercises" button from the lesson menu.

How can I recognize and remember the characters in each lesson?

Four character drill exercises are provided to reinforce your learning of each character:

In the first exercise, you are asked to click on the character that matches the meaning in English. You will not be able to move to the next question until you click on the correct character.

In the second exercise, you are asked to drag each character to the box that has the correct label. If you drag the character to the wrong box, the character will retract to where it started.

In the third exercise, you will find two parts that form a character. When you click on the correct parts, they will move to a location where the two meet. If you incorrectly identify the parts, nothing happens.

In the fourth exercise, you will find two parts that make up the simplified form of that character. This exercise allows you to compare how the traditional and simplified characters differ.

Stroke Orders

In this exercise, you can practice writing each character stroke by stroke and also control the timing of the movement of the strokes. Before practicing these exercises, you should print a few sheets of "hollow" characters from the "copybk" directory on the CD-ROM.

Pronunciation

When you click on the pronunciation menu, you can hear the correct pronunciation by a native speaker. Hearing the sound of the character also strengthens the connection with its meaning.

Phrases and Sentences

Four different kinds of exercises are available to reinforce your understanding of sentence structures and patterns.

In the first exercise, you are asked to recognize the compound word or phrase by clicking on the correct one.

In the second exercise, you are asked to fill in the blank of an incomplete sentence by clicking on one of the four alternatives. When you click on the correct answer, the word(s) will move to fill in the blank.

In the third exercise, you are asked to rearrange the sentence by dragging each sentence element to its correct position in the sentence.

In the fourth exercise, you are asked to translate an English sentence into a Chinese sentence by clicking, one by one, on the appropriate characters and punctuation marks that make up the sentence. When you click on the correct character, it will move to its assigned position.

What exercises do you provide for strengthening my listening skills?

Three exercises are included to help you develop better listening skills for characters, phrases, and sentences. These exercises, although different in content, follow basically the same format. First, listen to the sound, then determine the answer before it appears on the screen.

Tests

How can I determine if I have learned the material well enough?

You can take a test to see how well you have done. You can access the tests from the course menu, which is the first menu you see when opening the program. Each of the five tests covers the content of two lessons. These tests are not interactive, therefore, you should write down the answers on a sheet of paper. You can then score yourself by checking your answers with the answers at the end of the test. Assign two points to each correct answer. If your total score is 90 or better, you have done very well on the test. If you score below 70, you will benefit by reviewing and studying more before proceeding to the next lesson.

Course Dictionary

How can I use the course dictionary?

You can access the course dictionary from the course menu. The course dictionary provides a quick reference for each individual character. The characters are grouped according to the number of strokes. In addition to basic information, such as definition, simplified character, pinyin and zhuyin symbols, you can hear the pronunciation as well as view the stroking order for each character.

Phonetic Drills

Can I learn to pronounce the basic syllables in Chinese?

You can repeatedly listen to the pronunciation of the 21 initials (consonants) and 38 finals (vowels) in Mandarin by clicking on either the pinyin or zhuyin symbols.

How can I learn to distinguish the four tones?

You can listen to the tones of a syllable repeatedly by clicking on the tonal symbol in the tone section.

Other Questions

Is Chinese very difficult to learn?

In a strict sense, no language is easy to learn. Every language requires years of study and practice, and Chinese is no exception. In some respects, it is true that Chinese is among the more difficult-to-learn languages. But in other respects, Chinese is not as difficult as many people think. Hopefully with the learning system used in *Easy Chinese Tutor*, you will master the Chinese language quickly and comfortably.

Why do people believe that Chinese is difficult to learn?

The following are some major reasons why Chinese may be difficult to learn:

First, Chinese has no alphabet and, therefore, has no phonetic system of pronunciation. The pronunciation of Chinese words must be memorized by rote. Second, each Chinese character contains a number of arbitrary strokes that must be memorized and practiced. Third, there are many Chinese characters to learn. Fourth, since each character is a self-contained unit and is uniformly spaced, it is difficult to know how the characters should be combined and how they relate to each other in a sentence.

Can each individual Chinese characer be represented by a different sound?

The sounds of modern Chinese are limited in number. For this reason, many characters have the same sound but different tones. Thanks to pinyin, a scheme for the Chinese phonetic system, all the basic syllables in the common speech of modern Chinese can be represented by using the 26 letters of the English alphabet.

How can I remember the sounds and elements that make up all the characters?

Many Chinese characters consist of one or more basic elements known as radicals. A radical, which contains fewer strokes than the character itself, usually suggests the meaning of the character as a whole. When a radical is combined with another radical or a character, the latter often serves as a cue for the pronunciation of the character. Once you know how to write a radical and know the basic elements that make up a character, you can easily transfer your skill to the writing of other characters having the same radical or elements.

If I know the 800 or so most frequently used characters, will I be able to read modern Chinese with an adequate level of comprehension?

If you master these 800 characters, and related compound words, you should be able to read and write modern Chinese with about 80 percent communicative competence.

How can a vocabulary of only about 800 characters enable me to obtain such a level of proficiency?

This has a lot to do with the way characters can be combined to form disyllabic or trisyllabic words. One individual character may be a word in itself if it conveys a single concept or meaning. However, some characters may also be combined with another character (or sometimes even with the same character) to form a new word. Therefore, even though you have only learned about 800 characters, the actual number of words you have learned may exceed 5000 when compound words and phrases are included.

Is it true that you can substitute words in Chinese sentences more freely than those in the English language?

Nouns or pronouns can be interchanged in a Chinese sentence without regard to number or gender. Verbs remain unchanged whether the subject is singular or plural. Other substitutions are also possible because Chinese verbs are not conjugated.

Is it true that I must learn words by rote in the Chinese language to a far greater extent than in other languages?

Actually, the reverse is true. Because there are many visual and logical cues in the Chinese language, you can learn Chinese characters and words by taking advantage of your own abilities to visualize, to associate, and to reason.

Why is it difficult for a non-Chinese-speaking person to read Chinese?

Perhaps the most difficult problem for people who study Chinese as a second language is the way Chinese sentences appear on a printed page. Chinese characters are uniformly spaced without proper capitalization. It is difficult for beginners to know whether a character is related to the one before it or the one after it. It is also difficult to know which two characters join together to represent a separate word.

How can the problem of uniform spacing be overcome in learning Chinese?

One solution to the problem is to teach character combinations as soon as students have learned the appropriate characters as we do in *Easy Chinese*. Students should also be provided with numerous examples that show how characters in a sentence can relate to each other. This can be done by the use of boxes and diagrams, again as we do in this program.

Should I learn both traditional and simplified characters at the same time?

Unless you permanently stay in one place and read the same newspapers, it may be more advantageous for you to know both traditional and simplified characters. Actually, most of the characters in this first course are the same for both versions. In Mainland China, only simplified characters are taught in school. On the other hand, in Taiwan and in Hong Kong, students are primarily taught to read and write traditional characters. In the United States, most Chinese newspapers are printed in the traditional form. Although *Easy Chinese* places more emphasis on traditional characters, you can learn simplified characters at the same time with just a click of the mouse and a little extra effort.

Explanation of Lesson Format

Each lesson in this study course includes several base characters from which many compound words and phrases are formed. Each character set includes traditional and simplified characters, compound words or phrases, pinyin pronunciation guides, and definitions. Below is an example of a character set.

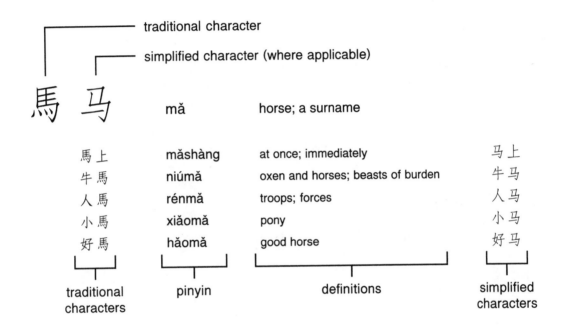

traditional character

simplified character (where applicable)

馬 马   mǎ   horse; a surname

馬上	mǎshàng	at once; immediately	马上
牛馬	niúmǎ	oxen and horses; beasts of burden	牛马
人馬	rénmǎ	troops; forces	人马
小馬	xiǎomǎ	pony	小马
好馬	hǎomǎ	good horse	好马

traditional characters   pinyin   definitions   simplified characters

Most of the lessons also include several illustrative sentences using words and phrases already introduced. Each set of sentences includes traditional characters, simplified characters, an English translation, and a pinyin pronunciation guide. Below is an example of an illustrative sentence set.

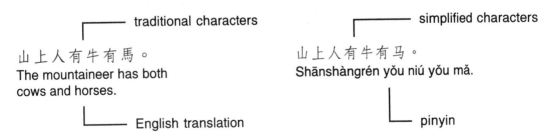

traditional characters

simplified characters

山上人有牛有馬。
The mountaineer has both cows and horses.

山上人有牛有马。
Shānshàngrén yǒu niú yǒu mǎ.

English translation

pinyin

第一課

Lesson 1

日	rì	sun; day	
日 日	rìrì	every day; daily	日 日
月	yuè	moon; month	
日 月	rìyuè	sun and moon; life; livelihood	日 月
山	shān	hill; mountain	
川	chuān	river; stream	
山 川	shānchuān	mountains and rivers; landscape	山 川

木　　　　mù　　　　tree; wood

土　　　　tǔ　　　　soil; earth; unrefined

土 木　　tǔmù　　　construction; civil engineering　　　土 木

水　　　　shuǐ　　　water; liquid

水 土　　shuǐtǔ　　water and soil; natural environment
　　　　　　　　　　and climate　　　　　　　　　　　　水 土
山 水　　shānshuǐ　water from mountain; landscape　　山 水

火　　　　huǒ　　　fire; anger; temper

火 山　　huǒshān　volcano　　　　　　　　　　　　　　火 山
水 火　　shuǐhuǒ　water and fire; incompatible　　　　水 火

上　　　　shàng　　above; up; go up

上 月　　shàngyuè　last month　　　　　　　　　　　　上 月
上 上　　shàngshàng　the very best　　　　　　　　　　上 上
上 山　　shàngshān　go up the mountain　　　　　　　　上 山

下	xià	below; under; next; descend	
下 月	xiàyuè	next month	下 月
下 山	xiàshān	go down a mountain	下 山
山 下	shānxià	below the mountain	山 下
上 上 下 下	shàngshàng-xiàxià	above and below; all; the whole	上 上 下 下

大	dà	big; large; great	
大 火	dàhuǒ	a big fire	大 火
大 水	dàshuǐ	flood	大 水
大 大	dàdà	greatly; enormously	大 大
大 月	dàyuè	a lunar month of 30 days	大 月
大 川	dàchuān	great river	大 川
大 山	dàshān	great mountain	大 山

小	xiǎo	little; small; minor; young	
小 小	xiǎoxiǎo	very small; a little bit	小 小
小 月	xiǎoyuè	a lunar month of 29 days	小 月
小 山	xiǎoshān	hill	小 山
小 川	xiǎochuān	small river	小 川
大 小	dàxiǎo	big or small; adults and children	大 小
月 小	yuèxiǎo	a lunar month of 29 days	月 小
大 大 小 小	dàdàxiǎoxiǎo	the big and the small; the whole family	大 大 小 小

Exercises Lesson 1

A. Identify the character that is related to each English concept.

1. big
   a. 天   b. 大   c. 人   d. 父

2. moon, month
   a. 白   b. 目   c. 月   d. 日

3. tree, wood
   a. 木   b. 母   c. 才   d. 本

4. water
   a. 小   b. 木   c. 來   d. 水

5. mountain
   a. 出   b. 尖   c. 山   d. 八

6. river, stream
   a. 川   b. 三   c. 不   d. 了

7. fire
   a. 夫   b. 火   c. 人   d. 炎

8. above
   a. 下   b. 今   c. 公   d. 上

9. soil
   a. 二   b. 它   c. 土   d. 六

10. small
    a. 小   b. 下   c. 四   d. 日

B. Identify the character that is associated with each pinyin transcription.

1. shàng
   a. 山   b. 三   c. 上   d. 川

2. huǒ
   a. 大　　　b. 火　　　c. 下　　　d. 日

3. shuǐ
   a. 木　　　b. 月　　　c. 水　　　d. 尖

4. yuè
   a. 月　　　b. 日　　　c. 目　　　d. 田

5. chuān
   a. 二　　　b. 天　　　c. 川　　　d. 山

C. Identify the pinyin transcription that is associated with each character.

1. 木
   a. dà　　　b. mǎ　　　c. mù　　　d. mú

2. 日
   a. rí　　　b. rī　　　c. rǐ　　　d. rì

3. 山
   a. shàng　　b. shān　　c. meǐ　　d. zhàng

4. 土
   a. tù　　　b. dú　　　c. tǔ　　　d. dǔ

5. 下
   a. xià　　　b. xiǎo　　c. shuì　　d. jiǎo

D. Identify the compound word or phrase that is associated with each English word
    or phrase.

1. livelihood
   a. 日月　　b. 大月　　c. 月小　　d. 上月

2. landscape
   a. 水月　　b. 山川　　c. 水土　　d. 大火

3. volcano
    a. 大水   b. 水火   c. 火山   d. 上火

4. the very best
    a. 大小   b. 上下   c. 大大   d. 上上

5. descend the mountain
    a. 下山   b. 上山   c. 上下   d. 山上

6. every day
    a. 日日   b. 月日   c. 日上   d. 小小

E. Identify the compound word or phrase that is associated with each pinyin transcription.

1. yuèdà
    a. 下月   b. 月下   c. 月大   d. 上月

2. dàchuān
    a. 山川   b. 大小   c. 山水   d. 大川

3. shānxià
    a. 山下   b. 上山   c. 大山   d. 上下

4. shuǐhuǒ
    a. 下水   b. 水月   c. 大水   d. 水火

5. dàshuǐ
    a. 大水   b. 大小   c. 下水   d. 大火

6. shàngxià
    a. 下山   b. 上下   c. 大小   d. 山下

F. Select the best choice.

1. Which of the following characters differs in tone from the others?
    a. 水   b. 火   c. 土   d. 山

2. Which of the following characters is pronounced in the fourth tone?
    a. 大   b. 土   c. 川   d. 小

3. Which of the following characters is pronounced in the first tone?
    a. 木   b. 下   c. 火   d. 川

4. Which of the following characters is pronounced in the third tone?
    a. 水   b. 日   c. 月   d. 大

5. Which of the following compound words consists of both characters in the same tone?
    a. 水月   b. 月小   c. 大月   d. 大火

6. Which of the following compound words consists of characters that are different in tone?
    a. 水火   b. 山川   c. 大水   d. 日月

Answers

A.	B.	C.	D.	E.	F.
1. b	1. c	1. c	1. a	1. c	1. d
2. c	2. b	2. d	2. b	2. d	2. a
3. a	3. c	3. b	3. c	3. a	3. d
4. d	4. a	4. c	4. d	4. d	4. a
5. c	5. c	5. a	5. a	5. a	5. c
6. a			6. a	6. b	6. c
7. b					
8. d					
9. c					
10. a					

第 二 課

Lesson 2

明　　　míng　　　bright; light; clear; next; obvious

明 日	míngrì	tomorrow; the near future	明 日
明 月	míngyuè	bright moon	明 月
明 明	míngmíng	obviously; undoubtedly	明 明

林　　　lín　　　forest; woods; grove; a surname

| 林 木 | línmù | woods; forest | 林 木 |
| 山 林 | shānlín | mountain and forest; wooded mountain | 山 林 |

森　　　sēn　　　full of trees; luxuriant vegetation; dark

| 森 林 | sēnlín | forest | 森 林 |
| 森 森 | sēnsēn | dense; thick | 森 森 |

炎　　　yán　　　very hot; scorching; burning

| 炎 炎 | yányán | very, very hot; scorching | 炎 炎 |

晶	jīng	brilliant; sparkling; radiant	
晶 晶	jīngjīng	particularly bright and brilliant	晶 晶
尖	jiān	point; tip; top; pointed; sharp	
山 尖	shānjiān	mountain top	山 尖
人	rén	a person; people	
人 人	rénrén	everybody; everyone	人 人
土 人	tǔrén	aborigines; natives	土 人
木 人	mùrén	dull person	木 人
大 人	dàrén	adult	大 人
小 人	xiǎorén	mean person	小 人
山 人	shānrén	hermit; mountaineer	山 人
口	kǒu	mouth; an opening	
人 口	rénkǒu	population	人 口
山 口	shānkǒu	mountain pass	山 口
口 水	kǒushuǐ	saliva	口 水

子   zǐ   child; son; seed; a suffix

口 子	kǒuzi	opening; hole; cut	口 子
日 子	rìzi	day; date; time; life	日 子
月 子	yuèzi	month of confinement after giving birth to a child	月 子
小 子	xiǎozi	young fellow; one's children	小 子
尖 子	jiānzǐ	cream of the crop	尖 子

女   nǔ   woman; female; daughter; girl

女 人	nǔrén	woman; one's wife	女 人
女 子	nǔzǐ	woman; girl; female	女 子
子 女	zǐnǔ	sons and daughters; children	子 女
下 女	xiànǔ	maid	下 女
小 女	xiǎonǔ	my daughter (a self-depreciatory term)	小 女

田   tián   field; farmland; a surname

| 水 田 | shuǐtián | rice field; paddy field | 水 田 |

目   mù   the eye; to look; to see

| 目 下 | mùxià | at present; right now | 目 下 |

好　　　　　　　hǎo　　　　　　good; fine; nice

好 人	hǎorén	good person; healthy person	好 人
好 大	hǎodà	How big!	好 大
好 日 子	hǎorìzi	good days; wedding day	好 日 子
好 小 子	hǎoxiǎozi	good boy	好 小 子

心　　　　　　　xīn　　　　　　　heart; mind; feeling

心 口	xīnkǒu	the pit of the stomach	心 口
心 目	xīnmù	mental view; frame of mind	心 目
心 田	xīntián	heart; intention	心 田
心 上	xīnshàng	in one's heart; in one's mind	心 上
人 心	rénxīn	public feeling; human heart	人 心
小 心	xiǎoxīn	be careful; take care	小 心
好 心	hǎoxīn	good intention; good will	好 心
心 上 人	xīnshàngrén	sweetheart	心 上 人
好 心 人	hǎoxīnrén	kind-hearted person	好 心 人

Exercises Lesson 2

A. Identify the character that is related to each English word.

   1.   people
        a. 明   b. 人   c. 口   d. 木

   2.   grove
        a. 林   b. 土   c. 森   d. 夫

   3.   heart
        a. 火   b. 心   c. 炎   d. 二

   4.   eye
        a. 日   b. 月   c. 目   d. 八

   5.   brilliant
        a. 品   b. 六   c. 出   d. 晶

   6.   bright
        a. 朋   b. 明   c. 炎   d. 四

   7.   field
        a. 口   b. 由   c. 田   d. 用

   8.   good
        a. 相   b. 她   c. 他   d. 好

   9.   son
        a. 字   b. 子   c. 入   d. 才

   10.   girl
        a. 女   b. 大   c. 行   d. 小

B. Identify the character that is related to each pinyin transcription.

   1.   rén
        a. 森   b. 木   c. 人   d. 炎

2. tián

   a. 火   b. 田   c. 林   d. 山

3. xīn

   a. 心   b. 森   c. 川   d. 三

4. hǎo

   a. 姐   b. 孕   c. 好   d. 女

5. mù

   a. 目   b. 四   c. 明   d. 每

6. kǒu

   a. 高   b. 可   c. 口   d. 中

C. Identify the pinyin transcription that is related to each character.

1. 炎

   a. dú   b. mǎ   c. yán   d. rán

2. 森

   a. shàng   b. shān   c. jìng   d. sēn

3. 明

   a. lín   b. míng   c. jiān   d. xià

4. 晶

   a. jīng   b. tián   c. xīn   d. liǎng

5. 尖

   a. zhàng   b. chuān   c. jiān   d. shuǐ

6. 子

   a. zǐ   b. nǔ   c. mù   d. yán

D. Identify the compound word or phrase that is related to each English concept.

1. forest
    a. 林木   b. 山林   c. 森林   d. 森森

2. tomorrow
    a. 明明   b. 明日   c. 明月   d. 日日

3. bright and brilliant
    a. 炎日   b. 明天   c. 月明   d. 晶晶

4. population
    a. 人字   b. 人口   c. 山人   d. 人人

5. hermit, mountaineer
    a. 山林   b. 山人   c. 山上   d. 尖子

6. children
    a. 女子   b. 小子   c. 子女   d. 下女

E. Identify the compound word or phrase that is related to each pinyin transcription.

1. shuǐtián
    a. 山水   b. 天上   c. 火山   d. 水田

2. mùxià
    a. 目下   b. 下雨   c. 下人   d. 月下

3. xiǎoxīn
    a. 小可   b. 小心   c. 小小   d. 好心

4. kǒuzi
    a. 人口   b. 口水   c. 口子   d. 尖子

5. kǒushuǐ
    a. 大水   b. 口水   c. 月子   d. 大口

6. rénxīn
    a. 人人   b. 好心   c. 人心   d. 中心

F.   Identify the character that is different in tone from the others.

1.   a. 水   b. 火   c. 好   d. 目

2.   a. 下   b. 上   c. 心   d. 日

3.   a. 山   b. 森   c. 炎   d. 晶

4.   a. 目   b. 月   c. 大   d. 林

5.   a. 土   b. 女   c. 子   d. 人

Answers

A.	B.	C.	D.	E.	F.
1. b	1. c	1. c	1. c	1. d	1. d
2. a	2. b	2. d	2. b	2. a	2. c
3. b	3. a	3. b	3. d	3. b	3. c
4. c	4. c	4. a	4. b	4. c	4. d
5. d	5. a	5. c	5. b	5. b	5. d
6. b	6. c	6. a	6. c	6. c	
7. c					
8. d					
9. b					
10. a					

第 三 課

Lesson 3

中   zhōng   middle; center; central; China

中 人	zhōngrén	middleman	中 人	
中 心	zhōngxīn	center	中 心	
心 中	xīnzhōng	in one's mind	心 中	

外   wài   outside; foreign; external

外 人	wàirén	outsiders; foreigners	外 人	
外 心	wàixīn	unfaithful intention	外 心	
外 子	wàizǐ	my husband	外 子	
中 外	zhōngwài	China and foreign countries	中 外	

牛   niú   ox; cow; buffalo; a surname

牛 心	niúxīn	the heart of an ox; stubbornness	牛 心	
水 牛	shuǐniú	buffalo	水 牛	
好 牛	hǎoniú	nice cow	好 牛	

馬 马　　**mǎ**　　horse; a surname

馬 上	**mǎshàng**	at once; immediately	马 上
牛 馬	**niúmǎ**	oxen and horses; beasts of burden	牛 马
人 馬	**rénmǎ**	troops; forces	人 马
小 馬	**xiǎomǎ**	pony	小 马
好 馬	**hǎomǎ**	good horse	好 马

也　　**yě**　　also; and; too

| 也 好 | **yěhǎo** | may as well; it may not be a bad idea | 也 好 |

門 门　　**mén**　　door; gate; entrance; family

門 人	**ménrén**	doorkeepers; disciples	门 人
門 口	**ménkǒu**	doorway; entrance	门 口
門 外	**ménwài**	outside the door	门 外
門 下	**ménxià**	disciple	门 下
大 門	**dàmén**	main entrance; main door	大 门
木 門	**mùmén**	wooden door	木 门

天　　**tiān**　　sky; heaven; day

| 天 明 | **tiānmíng** | dawn; daybreak | 天 明 |
| 天 下 | **tiānxià** | the world | 天 下 |

天 子	tiānzǐ	the emperor	天 子	
天 大	tiāndà	extremely big	天 大	
天 天	tiāntiān	every day	天 天	
天 上	tiānshàng	the sky	天 上	
天 外	tiānwài	outer space	天 外	
天 日	tiānrì	the sky and the sun	天 日	
明 天	míngtiān	tomorrow	明 天	
上 天	shàngtiān	God; Heaven	上 天	

地   dì   the earth; land; soil; ground

地 下	dìxià	underground	地 下	
地 上	dìshàng	on the ground	地 上	
地 心	dìxīn	center of the earth	地 心	
天 地	tiāndì	heaven and earth; universe	天 地	
土 地	tǔdì	land; soil	土 地	
田 地	tiándì	field; farmland	田 地	
地 下 水	dìxiàshuǐ	groundwater	地 下 水	

有   yǒu   to have; possess; exist; there is

有 心	yǒuxīn	intentionally	有 心	
有 人	yǒurén	some people; somebody	有 人	
有 心 人	yǒuxīnrén	a person who sets his/her mind on doing something	有 心 人	
有 日 子	yǒurìzi	to have arranged a date	有 日 子	

31

Illustrative Sentences

馬大川有子女。
Ma Dachuan has children.

马大川有子女。
Mǎ Dàchuān yǒu zǐnǔ.

門外有人。
There is somebody outside.

门外有人。
Ménwài yǒu rén.

馬月明有田有地。
Ma Yueming has both fields and land.

马月明有田有地。
Mǎ Yuèmíng yǒu tián yǒu dì.

山人有牛有馬。
The hermit has both cows and horses.

山人有牛有马。
Shānrén yǒu niú yǒu mǎ.

馬月明也有田有地。
Ma Yueming also has fields and land.

马月明也有田有地。
Mǎ yuèmíng yě yǒu tián yǒu dì.

山上人有牛有馬。
The mountaineer has both cows and horses.

山上人有牛有马。
Shānshàngrén yǒu niú yǒu mǎ.

| 沒 | méi | no; none; nothing | |
| | mò | sink; disappear | |

沒 有	méiyǒu	there is not; without; do not have	没 有
沒 人	méirén	nobody	没 人
沒 日 子	méirìzi	date not yet set	沒 日 子
沒 大 沒 小	méidàméixiǎo	ill-mannered to one's elders	没 大 没 小

門外有沒有人？
Is there someone outside?

门外有没有人？
Ménwài yǒu mei yǒu rén?

門外沒有人。
There is nobody outside.

门外没有人。
Ménwài méiyǒu rén.

山上沒有水。
There is no water on the mountain.

山上没有水。
Shānshàng méiyǒu shuǐ.

山人沒有子女。
The hermit does not have any children.

山人沒有子女。
Shānrén méiyǒu zǐnǚ.

馬大川沒有下人。
Ma Dachuan does not have a maid.

马大川没有下人。
Mǎ Dàchuān méiyǒu xiàrén.

是   shì   yes; correct; right; to be

是 日   shìrì   this day; that day   是 日

田也森是外地人。
Tian Yesen is from another region.

田也森是外地人。
Tián Yěsēn shì wàidìrén.

林小月是下人。
Lin Xiaoyue is a maid.

林小月是下人。
Lín Xiǎoyuè shì xiàrén.

山人是中山人。
The hermit is a native of Zhongshan.

山人是中山人。
Shānrén shì Zhōngshānrén.

子女也是人。
Children are people too.

子女也是人。
Zǐnǚ yě shì rén.

不   bù   no; not

不 是	búshì	is not	不 是
不 好	bùhǎo	not good; bad	不 好
不 明	bùmíng	not clear; do not understand	不 明
不 日	búrì	in a few days; soon	不 日
不 外	búwài	most likely; invariably	不 外

33

| 不 下 | búxià | not less than | 不 下 |
| 不 大 | búdà | not very; not often; not big | 不 大 |

林小月是不是下人？
Is Lin Xiaoyue a maid?

林小月是不是下人？
Lín xiǎoyuè shì bu shì xiàrén?

林小月不是下人。
Lin Xiaoyue is not a maid.

林小月不是下人。
Lín xiǎoyuè bú shì xiàrén.

山人是不是中山人？
Is the hermit a native of Zhongshan?

山人是不是中山人？
Shānrén shì bu shì Zhōngshānrén?

山人不是中山人。
The hermit is not a native of Zhongshan.

山人不是中山人。
Shānrén bú shì Zhōngshānrén.

田木森不是好人。
Tian Musen is a bad guy.

田木森不是好人。
Tián Mùsēn bú shì hǎorén.

Note: 不 becomes unstressed (i.e. bu) in a question form; it also changes to the second tone (i.e. bú) when the character after it is pronounced in the fourth tone.

夫

fū   husband; man; male adult; master

夫 人	fūren	Lady; Madame; Mrs.	夫 人
夫 子	fūzǐ	a title of respect for a scholar in ancient China	夫 子
大 夫	dàifu	doctor	大 夫
馬 夫	mǎfū	groom or stableman	马 夫

林大夫是好人。
Dr. Lin is a nice person.

林大夫是好人。
Lín dàifu shì hǎorén.

牛心田是馬夫。
Niu Xintian is a stableman.

牛心田是马夫。
Niú Xīntián shì mǎfū

林大夫是好心人。
Dr. Lin is a man of good intention.

林大夫是好心人。
Lín dàifu shì hǎoxīn rén.

馬小明是女大夫。
Ma Xiaoming is a female doctor.

马小明是女大夫。
Mǎ Xiǎomíng shì nǚ dàifu.

田大夫好不好？
Is Dr. Tian a good doctor? How is
Dr. Tian?

田大夫好不好？
Tián dàifu hǎo bu hǎo?

婦 妇	fù	woman; married woman; wife	
婦人	fùrén	woman; married woman; female	妇人
婦女	fùnǚ	women; females	妇女
夫婦	fū-fù	husband and wife	夫妇

林中明夫婦沒有子女。
Mr. and Mrs. Lin Zhongming do not
have any children.

林中明夫妇没有子女。
Lín Zhōngmíng fūfù méiyǒu zǐnǚ.

馬大川夫婦也沒有子女。
Ma Dachuan and his wife do not have
any children either.

马大川夫妇也没有子女。
Mǎ Dàchuān fūfù yě méiyǒu zǐnǚ.

林大夫是好婦人。
Dr. Lin is a nice woman.

林大夫是好妇人。
Lín dàifu shì hǎo fùrén.

馬大夫不是好婦人。
Dr. Ma is not a nice woman.

马大夫不是好妇人。
Mǎ dàifu bú shì hǎo fùrén.

35

家

jiā   family; house; home; a specialist in a certain field

家 人	jiārén	members of one's family	家 人
家 口	jiākǒu	the number of people in a family	家 口
家 門	jiāmén	social status of a family	家 门
家 小	jiāxiǎo	wife and children	家 小
人 家	rénjiā	household; other people	人 家
大 家	dàjiā	all of us; a famous expert	大 家
夫 家	fūjiā	husband's family	夫 家

田 大 夫 沒 有 家 人 。
Dr. Tian does not have any other family members.

田 大 夫 没 有 家 人 。
Tián dàifu méiyǒu jiārén.

馬 小 川 沒 有 家 。
Ma Xiaochuan does not have a family.

马 小 川 没 有 家 。
Mǎ Xiǎochuān méiyǒu jiā.

大 家 好 不 好 ？
How is everybody?

大 家 好 不 好 ？
Dàjiā hǎo bu hǎo?

家 人 好 不 好 ？
How is your family?

家 人 好 不 好 ？
Jiārén hǎo bu hǎo?

雨

yǔ   rain; rainy

雨 水	yǔshuǐ	rainwater	雨 水
下 雨	xiàyǔ	to rain	下 雨
大 雨	dàyǔ	heavy rain	大 雨
下 雨 天	xiàyǔtiān	rainy day	下 雨 天
下 大 雨	xiàdàyǔ	raining heavily	下 大 雨

山上有沒有下雨？
Did it rain on the mountain?

山上有没有下雨？
Shānshàng yǒu mei yǒu xià yǔ?

山上沒有下雨。
It did not rain on the mountain.

山上没有下雨。
Shānshàng méiyǒu xià yǔ.

山上下大雨。
It rained heavily on the mountain.

山上下大雨。
Shānshàng xià dà yǔ.

山上馬上下大雨。
A heavy rain is about to come on the mountain.

山上马上下大雨。
Shānshàng mǎshàng xià dà yǔ.

山上明明下大雨。
It is obviously raining heavily on the mountain.

山上明明下大雨。
Shānshàng míngmíng xià dà yǔ.

Exercises Lesson 3

A. Identify the character that is related to each English word.

1. middle
   a. 明　　　　b. 中　　　　c. 也　　　　d. 和

2. door
   a. 門　　　　b. 戶　　　　c. 森　　　　d. 生

3. horse
   a. 地　　　　b. 心　　　　c. 馬　　　　d. 力

4. outside
   a. 出　　　　b. 外　　　　c. 目　　　　d. 本

5. wife
   a. 品　　　　b. 父　　　　c. 母　　　　d. 婦

6. rain
   a. 法　　　　b. 雨　　　　c. 炎　　　　d. 水

7. home
   a. 家　　　　b. 長　　　　c. 了　　　　d. 品

8. cow
   a. 來　　　　b. 有　　　　c. 牛　　　　d. 力

9. also
   a. 字　　　　b. 合　　　　c. 也　　　　d. 在

10. sky
    a. 大　　　　b. 天　　　　c. 夫　　　　d. 中

B. Identify the character that is related to each pinyin transcription.

1. wài
   a. 決　　　　b. 外　　　　c. 人　　　　d. 表

2. yǒu
   a. 有   b. 田   c. 的   d. 可

3. dì
   a. 去   b. 林   c. 地   d. 它

4. yǔ
   a. 同   b. 雨   c. 兒   d. 以

5. niú
   a. 牛   b. 午   c. 才   d. 干

6. bù
   a. 他   b. 可   c. 不   d. 中

C. Identify the pinyin transcription that is related to each character.

1. 馬
   a. tò   b. mǎ   c. tián   d. jīng

2. 中
   a. chàng   b. jiān   c. jīn   d. zhōng

3. 家
   a. míng   b. lín   c. jiā   d. xià

4. 婦
   a. tàng   b. dián   c. xīn   d. fù

5. 是
   a. shàng   b. shì   c. chuān   d. shuǐ

6. 沒
   a. shuǐ   b. méi   c. mǔ   d. kán

D. Identify the compound word or phrase that is related to each English concept.

1. center
    a. 心中   b. 中文   c. 中午   d. 中心

2. to rain
    a. 明天   b. 下雨   c. 山下   d. 夫婦

3. everybody
    a. 人口   b. 上人   c. 大家   d. 好人

4. medical doctor
    a. 夫人   b. 大夫   c. 山人   d. 夫子

5. buffalo
    a. 牛馬   b. 牛心   c. 人馬   d. 水牛

6. husband and wife
    a. 夫人   b. 夫婦   c. 子女   d. 婦人

E. Identify the compound word or phrase that is related to each pinyin transcription.

1. tiándì
    a. 山地   b. 天地   c. 田地   d. 水田

2. dàyǔ
    a. 目下   b. 下雨   c. 大雨   d. 大水

3. bùhǎo
    a. 不好   b. 好人   c. 不是   d. 好心

4. ménwài
    a. 門人   b. 門口   c. 門外   d. 也門

5. daìfu
    a. 大水   b. 大夫   c. 大風   d. 地心

6. mǎshàng
    a. 牛馬   b. 馬上   c. 人馬   d. 上天

F. Identify the character that is different in tone from the others.

1. a. 大   b. 外   c. 日   d. 夫

2. a. 火   b. 牛   c. 馬   d. 土

3. a. 天   b. 田   c. 明   d. 人

4. a. 尖   b. 中   c. 夫   d. 婦

5. a. 不   b. 是   c. 沒   d. 月

6. a. 雨   b. 家   c. 好   d. 也

7. a. 下   b. 上   c. 門   d. 目

8. a. 有   b. 心   c. 川   d. 晶

G. Fill in the blanks with the appropriate words.

1. 馬明林—女人。
    a. 不   b. 有   c. 是   d. 下

2. 山人———家人？
    a. 明不明   b. 是不是   c. 有沒有   d. 大不大

3. 水牛有大有—。
    a. 上   b. 下   c. 馬   d. 小

4. 山下有——。
    a. 人家   b. 沒有   c. 日月   d. 月明

5. 林大牛——小人。
    a. 沒有   b. 不是   c. 不明   d. 好心

6. 森林———？
    a. 好不好   b. 有沒有   c. 大不大   d. 明不明

7. 子女 ——— ?
   a. 好不好   b. 有不有   c. 小沒小   d. 明好明

8. 天上有 —— 。
   a. 家人   b. 山川   c. 水火   d. 日月

H. Translate the following into English.

   1. 門外沒有人。

   2. 馬夫是外地人。

   3. 人有好有不好。

   4. 家人好不好?

   5. 門外明明下大雨。

   6. 馬大夫明明是好人。

I. Translate the following into Chinese.

   1. How is Dr. Lin?

   2. Is it raining heavily outside?

   3. The hermit does not have any children.

   4. Madame Ma is a good woman.

   5. Is Dr. Ma a native of Zhongshan?

Answers

A.	B.	C.	D.	E.
1. b	1. b	1. b	1. d	1. c
2. a	2. a	2. d	2. b	2. c
3. c	3. c	3. c	3. c	3. a
4. b	4. b	4. d	4. b	4. c
5. d	5. a	5. b	5. d	5. b
6. b	6. c	6. b	6. b	6. b
7. a				
8. c				
9. c				
10. b				

F.	G.
1. d	1. c
2. b	2. c
3. a	3. d
4. d	4. a
5. c	5. b
6. b	6. c
7. c	7. a
8. a	8. d

H.

1. There is nobody outside.
2. The groom is from another region.
3. There are good people and there are bad people.
4. How is your family?
5. Obviously it is raining heavily outside.
6. Dr. Ma is obviously a nice person.

I.

1. 林大夫好不好？
2. 門外是不是下大雨？
3. 山人沒有子女。
4. 馬夫人是好婦人
5. 馬大夫是不是中山人？

第四課

Lesson 4

一	yī	one; a; an; unit	
一家	yījiā	the same family	一家
一一	yīyī	one by one	一一
一口	yīkǒu	a mouthful	一口
一天	yītiān	one day in the past	一天
一下	yīxià	all of a sudden	一下
一心	yīxīn	wholeheartedly	一心
一日	yīrì	one day	一日
一月	yīyuè	January	一月
一下子	yīxiàzi	at once	一下子

二	èr	two	
一二	yī-èr	one or two; just a few	一二
二月	èryuè	February	二月

明天是一月一日。
Tomorrow is January the first.

明天是一月一日。
Míngtiān shì yīyuè yī rì.

二月一日是下雨天。
February 1 was a rainy day.

二月一日是下雨天。
Èryuè yī rì shì xiàyǔtiān.

馬大川一家明天上山。
Ma Dachuan and his family will
go up the mountain tomorrrow.

马大川一家明天上山。
Mǎ Dàchuān yījiā míngtiān shàng shān.

二月不是大月。
February is not a 31-day month.
(*lit.* February is not a large month.)

二月不是大月。
Èryuè bú shì dàyuè.

| 三 | sān | three | |
| | 三月　sānyuè | March | 三月 |

四	sì	four	
	四月　sìyuè	April	四月
	四川　sìchuān	Sichuan (Province)	四川
	不三不四　bùsān-búsì	dubious; shady in character	四川

明天是不是三月一日？
Is tomorrow the first day of March?

明天是不是三月一日？
Míngtiān shì bu shì sānyuè yī rì?

明天不是三月一日。
Tomorrow isn't March the first.

明天不是三月一日。
Míngtiān bú shì sānyuè yī rì.

林大夫是不是四川人？
Is Dr. Lin a native of Sichuan?

林大夫是不是四川人？
Lín dàifu shì bu shì Sìchuān rén?

林大夫是四川人。
Dr. Lin is a native of Sichuan.

林大夫是四川人。
Lín dàifu shì Sìchuān rén.

五   wǔ   five

五 月   wǔyuè   May   五 月

六   liù   six

六 月   liùyuè   June   六 月

五月天天下雨。
It rained every day in May.

五月天天下雨。
Wǔyuè tiāntiān xià yǔ.

五月不是小月。
May is not a month that has
30 days. (*lit.* May is not a small month.)

五月不是小月。
Wǔyuè bú shì xiǎo yuè.

山人六月六日下山。
The hermit will go down the mountain
on June 6.

山人六月六日下山。
Shānrén liùyuè liù rì xià shān.

山人六天沒有下山。
The hermit hasn't come down the
mountain for six days.

山人六天没有下山。
Shānrén liù tiān méiyǒu xià shān.

七   qī   seven

七 月   qīyuè   July   七 月

八　　　　　　　bā　　　　　eight

| 八 月 | bāyuè | August | 八 月 |
| 七 上 八 下 | qīshàng-bāxià | agitated; an unsettled state of mind | 七 上 八 下 |

七月沒有一天下雨。
It didn't rain at all in July.

七月沒有一天下雨。
Qīyuè méiyǒu yī tiān xià yǔ.

七月七日沒有下雨。
It didn't rain on July 7.

七月七日没有下雨。
Qīyuè qī rì méiyǒu xià yǔ.

八月八日是不是好日子？
Is August 8 an auspicious day?

八月八日是不是好日子？
Bāyuè bā rì shì bu shì hǎorìzi?

八月也是大月。
August is also a 31-day month.
(*lit.* August is the large month too.)

八月也是大月。
Bāyuè yě shì dà yuè.

九　　　　　　　jiǔ　　　　　nine

| 九 月 | jiǔyuè | September | 九 月 |

十　　　　　　shí　　　　　ten

十 月	shíyuè	October	十 月
十 一	shíyī	eleven	十 一
十 二	shí'èr	twelve	十 二
二 十	èrshí	twenty	二 十
三 十	sānshí	thirty	三 十
四 十	sìshí	forty	四 十
五 十	wǔshí	fifty	五 十
六 十	liùshí	sixty	六 十
七 十	qīshí	seventy	七 十
八 十	bāshí	eighty	八 十
九 十	jiǔshí	ninety	九 十
九 十 一	jiǔshíyī	ninety-one	九 十 一
十 一 月	shíyīyuè	November	十 一 月
十 二 月	shí'èryuè	December	十 二 月

十月有三十一天。
There are 31 days in October.

九月十三明明是下雨天。
September 13 was obviously a rainy day.

明天是八月十五。
Tomorrow is August 15.

山人六月二十五下山。
The hermit will come down from
the mountain on June 25.

十月有三十一天。
Shíyuè yǒu sānshíyī tiān.

九月十三明明是下雨天。
Jiǔyuè shísān míngmíng shì xiàyǔtiān.

明天是八月十五。
Míngtiān shì bāyuè shíwǔ.

山人六月二十五下山。
Shānrén liùyuè èrshíwǔ xià shān.

你　　　　　　nǐ　　　　　you (singular)

| 你 好 | nǐhǎo | How do you do? | 你 好 |

您　　　nín　　　a polite, formal form of 你

　　您好　　nínhǎo　　How do you do?　　　　　　　　您好

他　　　tā　　　he; him; other

　　他人　　tārén　　another person; other people　　他人
　　他日　　tārì　　someday; some other day　　　　他日

馬大夫，您好？
Dr. Ma, how do you do?

你有沒有子女？
Do you have any children?

你是不是四川人？
Are you a native of Sichuan?

他有沒有家人？
Does he have a family?
(*lit.* family person?)

他是不是林子明？
Is he Lin Ziming?

他不是林子明，他是馬大明。
He is not Lin Ziming; he is Ma Daming.

马大夫，您好？
Mǎ dàifu, nínhǎo?

你有没有子女？
Nǐ yǒu mei yǒu zǐnǚ?

你是不是四川人？
Nǐ shì bu shì Sìchuānrén?

他有没有家人？
Tā yǒu mei yǒu jiārén?

他是不是林子明？
Tā shì bu shì Lín Zǐmíng?

他不是林子明，他是马大明。
Tā bú shì Lín Zǐmíng; tā shì Mǎ Dàmíng.

我　　　wǒ　　　I; me; my; we; self

　　我家　　wǒjiā　　my family; my house; my home　　我家

們 们　　men　　a suffix that indicates the plural form of a word

人 們	rénmen	people; the public; men	人 们
你 們	nǐmen	you (plural); you all	你 们
他 們	tāmen	they; them	他 们
我 們	wǒmen	we; us	我 们

你有沒有子女？
Do you have any children?

你有没有子女？
Nǐ yǒu mei yǒu zǐnǔ?

我有一子一女。
I have a son and a daughter.

我有一子一女。
Wǒ yǒu yī zǐ yī nǔ.

我沒有子女。
I don't have any children.

我没有子女。
Wǒ méiyǒu zǐnǔ.

你們是不是外地人？
Are you all (plural) from another region?

你们是不是外地人？
Nǐmen shì bu shì wàidìrén?

我們不是外地人；
我們也是四川人。
We're not from another region;
we too are Sichuan natives.

我们不是外地人；
我们也是四川人。
Wǒmen bú shì wàidìrén,
wǒmen yě shì Sìchuānrén.

她　　tā　　she; her

她 們	tāmen	they (plural of she)	她 们

它　　tā　　it

它 們	tāmen	they (plural of it)	它 们

她們是不是女大夫？
Are they female doctors?

她们是不是女大夫？
Tāmen shì bu shì nǚ dàifu?

她們不是大夫，她們是下女。
They aren't doctors; they are maids.

她们不是大夫，她们是下女。
Tāmen bú shì dàifū, tāmen shì xiànǔ.

她們是不是好女人？
Are they nice women?

她们是不是好女人？
Tāmen shì bu shì hǎo nǚrén?

她們是好女人。
They are nice women.

她们是好女人。
Tāmen shì hǎo nǚrén.

的	de	a word that is used to indicate possession	
是 的	shìde	yes; right	是 的
有 的	yǒude	some	有 的
好 的	hǎode	good!; O.K.	好 的
目 的	mùde	objective; goal; purpose	目 的
好 好 的	hǎohǎode	perfectly all right	好 好 的
有 的 是	yǒudeshì	to have plenty of	有 的 是

了	le	a word that is used to indicate the completion of an action or some changes in the current situation	
	liǎo	to finish; to understand	
明 了	míngliǎo	understand; be clear about	明 了
有 了	yǒule	to grasp an idea	有 了
好 了	hǎole	that's enough!	好 了

她 不 是 我 的 大 夫 。
She isn't my doctor.

他 們 是 我 的 子 女 。
They are my children.

他 是 不 三 不 四 的 人 。
He is a person of dubious character.

不 好 了 。
Something bad is happening!

下 雨 了 。
It's raining now.

他 們 不 是 好 夫 婦 了 。
They're no longer a nice married couple.

她 不 是 我 的 大 夫 。
Tā bú shì wǒ de dàifu.

他 们 是 我 的 子 女 。
Tāmen shì wǒ de zǐnǔ.

他 是 不 三 不 四 的 人 。
Tā shì bùsān-bùsì de rén.

不 好 了 。
Bù hǎo le.

下 雨 了 。
Xià yǔ le.

他 们 不 是 好 夫 妇 了 。
Tāmen bú shì hǎo fūfù le.

去	qù	to go; leave; depart; past	
去 了	qùle	already gone	去 了
上 去	shàngqu	go up	上 去
下 去	xiàqu	go down	下 去
去 不 了	qùbùliǎo	unable to go	去 不 了
去 不 去	qùbuqù	(Are you) going? (used for questioning)	去 不 去

出	chū	to go out; to come out	
出 門	chūmén	go out; be away from home	出 门
出 家	chūjiā	become a monk or nun	出 家
出 口	chūkǒu	exit; export; talk	出 口

出 馬	chūmǎ	take charge of the matter	出 马
出 沒	chūmò	appear and disappear	出 没
出 去	chūqu	go out; get out	出 去
出 土	chūtǔ	come up out of the ground	出 土
出 外	chūwài	leave for a distant place	出 外
日 出	rìchū	sunrise	日 出
出 家 人	chūjiārén	a monk or a nun	出 家 人

你明天去不去中山？
Are you going to Zhongshan tomorrow?

你明天去不去中山？
Nǐ míngtiān qù bu qù Zhōngshān?

我明天不去中山了。
I am not going to Zhongshan tomorrow (as planned.)

我明天不去中山了。
Wǒ míngtiān bú qù Zhōngshān le.

你明天出門不出門？
Will you go out (leave home) tomorrow?

你明天出门不出门？
Nǐ míngtiān chūmen bu chūmen?

我明天不出門。
I will not go out tomorrow.

我明天不出门。
Wǒ míngtiān bù chūmen.

他有沒有出去？
Did he go out?

他有没有出去？
Tā yǒu mei yǒu chūqù?

沒有，他沒有出去。
No, he didn't go out.

没有，他没有出去。
Méiyǒu, tā méiyǒu chūqù.

53

Exercises Lesson 4

A. Identify the character that is related to the English word(s) or phrase.

1. four
    a. 馬   b. 心   c. 也   d. 四

2. nine
    a. 父   b. 戶   c. 九   d. 本

3. you
    a. 它   b. 你   c. 他   d. 力

4. I, me
    a. 我   b. 方   c. 位   d. 久

5. she
    a. 他   b. 們   c. 也   d. 她

6. particle
    a. 妹   b. 家   c. 的   d. 好

7. go, leave
    a. 可   b. 去   c. 目   d. 晶

8. seven
    a. 全   b. 八   c. 七   d. 土

9. ten
    a. 字   b. 十   c. 木   d. 三

10. to go out
    a. 出   b. 來   c. 五   d. 同

B. Identify the character that is related to each pinyin transcription.

1. de
    a. 了   b. 的   c. 它   d. 十

2. wǒ
   a. 我   b. 和   c. 們   d. 你

3. sì
   a. 去   b. 四   c. 三   d. 六

4. èr
   a. 三   b. 二   c. 五   d. 九

5. nǐ
   a. 牛   b. 它   c. 你   d. 她

6. qù
   a. 出   b. 可   c. 外   d. 去

C. Identify the pinyin transcription that is related to each character.

1. 出
   a. qú   b. nǎ   c. tián   d. chū

2. 五
   a. háng   b. tān   c. wǔ   d. hōng

3. 十
   a. shí   b. míng   c. shān   d. men

4. 去
   a. qīng   b. tiān   c. xīn   d. qù

5. 他
   a. xià   b. shì   c. tā   d. shuǐ

6. 一
   a. yī   b. sān   c. bù   d. shān

D. Identify the compound word or phrase that is related to the English word(s) or phrase.

1. February
    a. 一月   b. 一二   c. 二月   d. 一日

2. fifty
    a. 三十   b. 十五   c. 十九   d. 五十

3. August
    a. 八月   b. 七月   c. 四月   d. 十月

4. we
    a. 人們   b. 她們   c. 我們   d. 門人

5. yes, right
    a. 不是   b. 的了   c. 是的   d. 沒有

6. to go out
    a. 去了   b. 出門   c. 出口   d. 出去

E. Identify the compound word or phrase that is related to each pinyin transcription.

1. rìchū
    a. 日出   b. 大地   c. 出門   d. 有日

2. sānyuè
    a. 山尖   b. 下雨   c. 三月   d. 四十

3. yījiā
    a. 一心   b. 出家   c. 家人   d. 一家

4. liùshíwǔ
    a. 五十六   b. 六十五   c. 八十三   d. 三十五

5. nǐhǎo
    a. 女子   b. 不好   c. 你好   d. 好心

6. yǒude
    a. 沒有   b. 外地   c. 有的   d. 它的

F. Identify the character that is different in tone from the others.

1. a. 一   b. 天   c. 三   d. 四

2. a. 我   b. 你   c. 馬   d. 她

3. a. 十   b. 田   c. 明   d. 們

4. a. 去   b. 中   c. 八   d. 它

5. a. 出   b. 七   c. 十   d. 三

6. a. 她   b. 家   c. 九   d. 川

7. a. 六   b. 七   c. 二   d. 下

8. a. 有   b. 五   c. 了   d. 好

G. Fill in the blanks with the appropriate words or phrases.

1. 他五月一日—四川。
   a. 出   b. 的   c. 去   d. 下

2. 你明天 ———中山？
   a. 去不去   b. 出不出   c. 有沒有   d. 好不好

3. 明天是他—好日子。
   a. 了   b. 有   c. 的   d. 沒

4. ——是一家人。
   a. 家中   b. 它們   c. 有人   d. 我們

5. 馬小明是不是——家人。
   a. 他的   b. 有心   c. 不大   d. 大家

6. 他們———子女？
   a. 好不好   b. 有沒有   c. 大不大   d. 是不是

7. 她們是不是 —— 去了？
    a. 山上   b. 出沒   c. 出門   d. 大家

8. 明天不是 —— 十五。
    a. 日子   b. 下月   c. 日日   d. 八月

H. Rearrange the word groups to form meaningful sentences.

1. 是，四川人，他的，大夫。

2. 去不去，你，中山，明天？

3. 下雨天，十三，是，四月。

4. 了，上山，她，去。

5. 沒有，他，出去，有？

6. 你的，大，牛，不大？

I. Translate the following into English.

1. 明天是不是六月二十一日？

2. 你是不是四川人？

3. 五月九日沒有下雨。

4. 她們出去了。

5. 你的馬大不大？

J. Translate the following into Chinese.

    1.   How are you?

    2.   She is my maid.

    3.   She isn't a medical doctor.

    4.   I understand now.

    5.   He is a monk.

Answers

A.	B.	C.	D.	E.
1. d	1. b	1. d	1. c	1. a
2. c	2. a	2. c	2. d	2. c
3. b	3. b	3. a	3. a	3. d
4. a	4. b	4. d	4. c	4. b
5. d	5. c	5. c	5. c	5. c
6. c	6. d	6. a	6. d	6. c
7. b				
8. c				
9. b				
10. a				

F.	G.	H.
1. d	1. c	1. 他的大夫是四川人。
2. d	2. a	2. 你明天去不去中山？
3. d	3. c	3. 四月十三是下雨天。
4. a	4. d	4. 她上山去了。
5. c	5. a	5. 他有沒有出去？
6. c	6. b	6. 你的牛大不大？
7. b	7. c	
8. c	8. d	

I.

1. Is tomorrow June 21?
2. Are you a native of Sichuan?
3. It didn't rain on May 9.
4. They are out.
5. Is your horse big?

J.

1. 你好。
2. 她是我的下人。
3. 她不是大夫。
4. 我明了。
5. 他是出家人。

第五課

Lesson 5

今   jīn   now; present; current

今 日   jīnrì   today; nowadays   今 日

今 天   jīntiān   today   今 天

來   lái   come; arrive

來 人   láirén   the person who came; the messenger   来 人

來 日   láirì   tomorrow; the future   来 日

今天是不是他們的好日子？
Is today their wedding (good) day?

今天是不是他们的好日子？
Jīntiān shì bu shì tāmen de hǎorìzi?

不是今天；是明天。
It isn't today; it's tomorrow.

不是今天；是明天。
Bú shì jīntiān; shì míngtiān.

他今天來我家。
He came to my home today.

他今天来我家。
Tā jīntiān lái wǒ jiā.

她今天上山。
She is going up/coming up the mountain today.

她今天上山。
Tā jīntiān shàng shān.

她今天上山來。
She is coming up the mountain today.

她今天上山来。
Tā jīntiān shàng shān lái.

她今天上山去。
She is going up the mountain today.

她今天上山去。
Tā jīntiān shàng shān qù.

她今天上山來了。
She came up the mountain today.

她今天上山来了。
Tā jīntiān shàng shān lái le.

昨　　　　zuó　　　　yesterday

昨 天　　zuótiān　　yesterday　　　　　　　　　　昨 天
昨 日　　zuórì　　　yesterday　　　　　　　　　　昨 日

前　　　　qián　　　front; forward; ahead; before; previous

前 夫　　qiánfu　　　ex-husband　　　　　　　　　前 夫
前 門　　qiánmén　　front door　　　　　　　　　　前 门
前 人　　qiánrén　　people of the past　　　　　　前 人
前 日　　qiánrì　　　the day before yesterday　　　前 日
前 天　　qiántiān　　the day before yesterday　　　前 天

你昨天有沒有出去？
Did you go out yesterday?

你昨天有没有出去？
Nǐ zuótiān yǒu mei yǒu chūqu?

有，我去小田家。
Yes, I went to Xiaotian's home.

有，我去小田家。
Yǒu, wǒ qù Xiǎotián jiā.

田大川是她的前夫。
Tian Dachuan is her ex-husband.

田大川是她的前夫。
Tián Dàchuān shì tā de qiánfu.

前天是不是下雨天？
Was the day before yesterday a
rainy day?

前天是不是下雨天？
Qiántiān shì bu shì xiàyǔtiān?

朋　　　　péng　　　　friend; companion

友　　　　yǒu　　　　friend; friendly; friendship

朋友	péngyou	friend	朋友
友人	yǒurén	friend	友人
友好	yǒuhǎo	friendly; close friend	友好
好朋友	hǎopéngyou	good friend	好朋友
女朋友	nǚpéngyou	girlfriend	女朋友

她是我的好朋友。
He is my good friend.

她是我的好朋友。
Tā shì wǒ de hǎo péngyou.

我們是好朋友。
We are good friends.

我们是好朋友。
Tā shì wǒ de hǎo péngyou.

她不是我的女朋友。
She isn't my girlfriend.

她不是我的女朋友。
Tā bú shì wǒ de nǚpéngyou.

我沒有女朋友。
I don't have a girlfriend.

我没有女朋友。
Wǒ méiyǒu nǚpéngyou.

他們不友好。
They aren't on good terms.

他们不友好。
Tāmen bù yǒuhǎo.

看　　　　　kàn　　　　　see; look at; visit; read; treat

看 出	kànchū	detect		看 出
看 來	kànlái	it appears; it seems		看 来
看 看	kànkàn	take a look at		看 看
看 人	kànrén	see or visit someone		看 人
看 上	kànshang	be satisfied with		看 上
看 中	kànzhòng	like; settle on		看 中
好 看	hǎokàn	good-looking; interesting		好 看
看 一 看	kànyīkàn	take a look		看 一 看
看 不 出	kànbuchū	unable to detect		看 不 出

在　　　　　zài　　　　　at; in; on; exist; be living; be present

在 家	zàijiā	be at home		在 家
在 外	zàiwài	outside		在 外
在 我	zàiwǒ	up to me		在 我
在 下	zàixià	my humble self		在 下
在 在	zàizài	everywhere		在 在
在 心	zàixīn	attentive		在 心
不 在	búzài	not to be in		不 在
好 在	hǎozài	luckily; fortunately		好 在

我昨天去看朋友。
I went to see a friend yesterday.

我 昨 天 去 看 朋 友 。
Wǒ zuótiān qù kàn péngyou.

你有沒有去看大夫？
Did you go to see a doctor?

你 有 没 有 去 看 大 夫 ？
Nǐ yǒu mei yǒu qù kàn dàifu?

他看來不是好人。
He looks like a bad person.

他看来不是好人。
Tā kànlái bú shì hǎorén.

我看出他不是好人。
I can tell that he is not a good person.

我看出他不是好人。
Wǒ kànchū tā bú shì hǎorén.

馬中明的女朋友不好看。
Ma Zhongming's girlfriend is not attractive.

马中明的女朋友不好看。
Mǎ Zhōngmíng de nǚpéngyou bù hǎokàn.

他昨天來看我，我不在家。
He came to see me yesterday, (but) I wasn't at home.

他昨天来看我，我不在家。
Tā zuótiān lái kàn wǒ, wǒ bú zài jiā.

她在門口。
She is at the door.

她在门口。
Tā zài ménkǒu.

他不在了。
He is dead. (*lit.* He is no longer in.)

他不在了。
Tā bú zài le.

我在看日出。
I am watching the sun rising.

我在看日出。
Wǒ zài kàn rìchū.

林大夫在看他。
Dr. Lin is examining him.

林大夫在看他。
Lín dàifu zài kàn tā.

晚	wǎn	evening; night; late	
晚來	wǎnlái	come late	晚来
晚了	wǎnle	already late	晚了
晚上	wǎnshang	at night; in the evening	晚上
今晚	jīnwǎn	tonight	今晚
昨晚	zuówǎn	last night	昨晚
前晚	qiánwǎn	the evening before last	前晚

65

嗎 吗　　ma　　　　a word that is used for questioning

今天晚上有人來看我。
Somebody will come to see me tonight.

今 天 晚 上 有 人 来 看 我 。
Jīntiān wǎnshang yǒu rén lái kàn wǒ.

他昨晚不在家。
He wasn't at home last night.

他 昨 晚 不 在 家 。
Tā zuówǎn bú zài jiā.

我今晚不出去。
I am not going out tonight.

我 今 晚 不 出 去 。
Wǒ jīnwǎn bù chūqu.

你今晚在家嗎？
Will you be home tonight?

你 今 晚 在 家 吗 ？
Nǐ jīnwǎn zài jiā ma?

她有子女嗎？
Does she have any children?

她 有 子 女 吗 ？
Tā yǒu zǐnǚ ma?

她是你的女朋友嗎？
Isn't she your girlfriend?

她 是 你 的 女 朋 友 吗 ？
Tā shì nǐ de nǚpéngyou ma?

馬大夫看他嗎？
Is Dr. Ma going to see/treat him?

马 大 夫 看 他 吗 ？
Mǎ dàifu kàn tā ma?

你好嗎？
How are you?

你 好 吗 ？
Nǐ hǎo ma?

早　　　　zǎo　　　　early; soon; morning

早 日	zǎorì	at an earlier day	早 日
早 上	zǎoshang	early in the morning	早 上
早 晚	zǎowǎn	sooner or later; morning and evening	早 晚
一 早	yīzǎo	early in the morning	一 早

回　　　huí　　　return; go back; reply; answer

回 來	huílai	return; come back	回 来
回 去	huíqu	go back	回 去
回 家	huíjiā	go home	回 家
回 門	huímén	a bride's first visit to her parents' home	回 门

你明天回家嗎？
Will you return home tomorrow?

你明天回家吗？
Nǐ míngtiān huí jiā ma?

我今晚不回家。
I will not come home tonight.

我今晚不回家。
Wǒ jīnwǎn bù huíjiā.

她早上出去，晚上回來。
She went out in the morning and returned at night.

她早上出去，晚上回来。
Tā zǎoshang chūqu, wǎnshang huíjiā.

你今晚回來嗎？
Will you be back tonight?

你今晚回来吗？
Nǐ jīnwǎn huílái ma?

你今晚回來不回來？
Will you come back tonight?

你今晚回来不回来？
Nǐ jīnwǎn huílái bu huílái?

我今晚不回來。
I will not come back tonight.

我今晚不回来。
Wǒ jīnwǎn bù huílái.

我明天早上回來。
I will come back early in the morning tomorrow.

我明天早上回来。
Wǒ míngtiān zǎoshang huílái.

Exercises   Lesson 5

A.   Identify the character that is related to each English concept or phrase.

1.   to come
a. 目   b. 光   c. 全   d. 來

2.   to return
a. 合   b. 回   c. 白   d. 行

3.   today
a. 今   b. 年   c. 加   d. 也

4.   early
a. 開   b. 方   c. 早   d. 利

5.   to see
a. 出   b. 看   c. 兵   d. 本

6.   friend
a. 朋   b. 明   c. 朗   d. 高

7.   late
a. 平   b. 次   c. 每   d. 晚

8.   to be at
a. 生   b. 在   c. 去   d. 世

9.   before, ahead
a. 字   b. 長   c. 前   d. 外

10.   a word used to form a question
a. 嗎   b. 媽   c. 碼   d. 罵

B.   Identify the character that is related to each pinyin transcription.

1.   huí
a. 去   b. 的   c. 回   d. 七

2. yǒu
    a. 友   b. 和   c. 朋   d. 沒

3. jīn
    a. 五   b. 四   c. 十   d. 今

4. zài
    a. 在   b. 土   c. 四   d. 口

5. zuó
    a. 出   b. 昨   c. 地   d. 來

6. qián
    a. 前   b. 他   c. 朋   d. 尖

7. ma
    a. 八   b. 它   c. 目   d. 嗎

8. lái
    a. 看   b. 來   c. 川   d. 去

C. Identify the pinyin transcription that is related to each character.

1. 朋
    a. pèng   b. pēng   c. péng   d. pěng

2. 今
    a. jín   b. jīn   c. jǐn   d. jìn

3. 回
    a. huī   b. huí   c. huǐ   d. huì

4. 早
    a. zào   b. zǎo   c. zāo   d. záo

5. 看
    a. kàn   b. kǎn   c. kān   d. kán

6. 晚
    a. wàn   b. wǎn   c. wān   d. wán

D. Identify the compound word or phrase that is related to each English phrase or concept.

1. go back
    a. 回家　　　b. 回去　　　c. 出去　　　d. 出來

2. today
    a. 明天　　　b. 日子　　　c. 今天　　　d. 有日

3. yesterday
    a. 昨天　　　b. 前日　　　c. 今日　　　d. 來日

4. in the evening
    a. 晚來　　　b. 前晚　　　c. 晚了　　　d. 晚上

5. it seems
    a. 看來　　　b. 看了　　　c. 好看　　　d. 看上

6. friend
    a. 看人　　　b. 來人　　　c. 朋友　　　d. 在外

E. Identify the compound word or phrase that is related to each pinyin transcription.

1. huíjiā
    a. 在家　　　b. 大家　　　c. 出門　　　d. 回家

2. hǎozài
    a. 好人　　　b. 好在　　　c. 在下　　　d. 好看

3. zǎoshang
    a. 一早　　　b. 晚上　　　c. 早上　　　d. 來日

4. qiánmén
    a. 前門　　　b. 門口　　　c. 前人　　　d. 門外

5. zàixīn
    a. 有心　　　b. 不好　　　c. 在心　　　d. 好心

6. jīnwǎn
    a. 今日　　　b. 今晚　　　c. 晚上　　　d. 昨晚

F. Identify the character that is different in tone from the others.

1. a. 今   b. 大   c. 上   d. 四

2. a. 明   b. 你   c. 人   d. 來

3. a. 在   b. 田   c. 昨   d. 朋

4. a. 家   b. 山   c. 前   d. 它

5. a. 晚   b. 我   c. 好   d. 嗎

6. a. 看   b. 九   c. 友   d. 馬

7. a. 外   b. 回   c. 目   d. 下

8. a. 有   b. 早   c. 出   d. 好

G. Fill in the blanks with the appropriate words or phrases.

1. 我今天——出門。
a. 在心   b. 一早   c. 看看   d. 下山

2. 她是你的——嗎？
a. 朋友   b. 外子   c. 水牛   d. 前人

3. 今天是——十五。
a. 上月   b. 下月   c. 八月   d. 月大

4. 我昨天去—林大夫。
a. 出   b. 看   c. 早   d. 在

5. 他的女朋友昨天——回家。
a. 不是   b. 沒有   c. 出來   d. 看來

6. 昨晚我——沒有出去。
a. 好在   b. 好心   c. 在在   d. 在下

7.　有人 —— 嗎 ？
　　a. 看看　　b. 早晚　　c. 在家　　d. 在看

8.　—— 是他們的好日子。
　　a. 早上　　b. 晚上　　c. 日日　　d. 今天

H.　Rearrange the word groups to form meaningful sentences.

1.　沒有，朋友，他的，來 。

2.　晚上，我，在家，不 。

3.　她，沒有，了，回來 ？

4.　嗎，是，好人，他 ？

5.　不是，今天，二十，五月 。

6.　她，看我，來，晚上 。

7.　他們，回去，今天，不 。

I.　Translate the following into English.

1.　昨天是不是下雨天 ？

2.　我沒有女朋友。

3.　你明天在家嗎 ？

4.　昨天有沒有下雨 ？

5.　她的前夫前天去看她。

6.　他的女朋友好看嗎 ？

J.   Translate the following into Chinese.

   1.   She has a son and a daughter.

   2.   I will go to see her in the morning tomorrow.

   3.   His girlfriend is not attractive.

   4.   He will go to see Dr. Lin tomorrow.

   5.   She was not at home yesterday.

   6.   How are your children?

Answers

A.	B.	C.	D.	E.
1. d	1. c	1. c	1. b	1. d
2. b	2. a	2. b	2. c	2. b
3. a	3. d	3. b	3. a	3. c
4. c	4. a	4. b	4. d	4. a
5. b	5. b	5. a	5. a	5. c
6. a	6. a	6. b	6. c	6. b
7. d	7. d			
8. b	8. b			
9. c				
10. a				

F.	G.	H.
1. a	1. b	1. 他的朋友沒有來。
2. b	2. a	2. 我晚上不在家。
3. a	3. c	3. 她回來了沒有？
4. c	4. b	4. 他是好人嗎？
5. d	5. b	5. 今天不是五月二十。
6. a	6. a	6. 她晚上來看我。
7. b	7. c	7. 他們今天不回去。
8. c	8. d	

I.

1. Was yesterday a rainy day?
2. I don't have a girlfriend.
3. Will you be home tomorrow?
4. Did it rain yesterday?
5. Her ex-husband went to see her the day before yesterday.
6. Is his girlfriend attractive?

J.

1. 她有一子一女。
2. 我明天早上去看她。
3. 他的女朋友不好看。
4. 他明天去看林大夫。
5. 她昨天不在家。
6. 你的子女好嗎？

第 六 課
Lesson 6

很   hěn   very; quite

亮   liàng   bright; light; clear; enlightened

月 亮	yuèliang	moon	月 亮
明 亮	míngliàng	bright; light; shining	明 亮
天 亮	tiānliàng	dawn; daybreak	天 亮

他 的 女 朋 友 很 好 看。
His girlfriend is very attractive.

他 的 女 朋 友 很 好 看。
Tā de nǚpéngyou hěn hǎo kàn.

他 的 心 地 很 好。
He has a very kind heart.

他 的 心 地 很 好。
Tā de xīndì hěn hǎo.

我 昨 天 很 晚 回 家。
I came home very late yesterday.

我 昨 天 很 晚 回 家。
Wǒ zuótiān hěn wǎn huíjiā.

他 的 水 牛 很 大。
His buffalo is very big.

他 的 水 牛 很 大。
Tā de shuǐniú hěn dà.

75

我今天很早出來。
I came out very early today.

我今天很早出来。
Wǒ jīntiān hěn zǎo chūlai.

天亮了。
It's light already.

天亮了。
Tiān liàng le.

今晚月亮看來很大。
The moon appears very big tonight.

今晚月亮看来很大。
Jīnwǎn yuèliàng kànlái hěn dá.

每		měi	every; each; per		
每 每		měiměi	often	每 每	
每 天		měitiān	every day; daily	每 天	
每 人		měirén	everybody; everyone	每 人	
每 日		měirì	daily; every day	每 日	
每 月		měiyuè	every month; monthly	每 月	

都		dōu	all; together; already		
都 是		dōushì	all; without exception	都 是	
都 有		dōuyǒu	all have	都 有	
都 來 了		dōuláile	all are here; everyone is here	都 来 了	
都 不 是		dōubúshì	none is	都 不 是	
不 都 是		bùdōushì	not all are	不 都 是	

他每每不在家。
He is often not at home.

他每每不在家。
Tā měiměi bú zài jiā.

他每天一早出門。
He leaves home very early every day.

他每天一早出门。
Tā měitiān yīzǎo chūmén.

他每三天來我家。
He comes to my home every three days.

他每三天来我家。
Tā měi sān tiān lái wǒ jiā.

他們都是四川人。
They are all Sichuanians.

他们都是四川人。
Tāmen dōu shì Sìchuānrén.

我們都有女朋友。
We all have girlfriends.

我们都有女朋友。
Wǒmen dōu yǒu nǔpéngyou.

大家都來了。
Everybody is here.

大家都来了。
Dàjiā dōu lái le.

誰 谁   shuí (shéi)   who; anyone

誰 的   shuíde   whose   谁 的
誰 家   shuíjiā   which family; which household   谁 家
誰 人   shuírén   who   谁 人

國 国   guó   country; state; nation

國 家   guójiā   country; nation   国 家
國 門   guómén   the gateway of a country 国 门
國 人   guórén   fellow countrymen   国 人
國 土   guótǔ   territory of a country   国 土
國 有   guóyǒu   state-owned   国 有
中 國   zhōngguó   China   中 国

誰是他的女朋友？
Who is his girlfriend?

谁是他的女朋友？
Shuí shì tā de nǔpéngyou?

她是誰的女朋友？
Whose girlfriend is she?

她是谁的女朋友？
Tā shì shuí de nǚpéngyou?

你們誰有女朋友？
Do any one of you have a girlfriend?

你们谁有女朋友？
Nǐmen shuí yǒu nǚpéngyou?

他們都是中國人。
They are all Chinese.

他们都是中国人。
Tāmen dōu shì Zhōngguórén.

中國有很大的國土。
China has very large territories.

中国有很大的国土。
Zhōngguó yǒu hěn dà de guótǔ.

我國有很大的森林。
Our country has very big forests.

我國有很大的森林。
Wǒguó yǒu hěn dà de sēnlín.

我們明天去中國。
We are going to China tomorrow.

我们明天去中国。
Wǒmen míngtiān qù Zhōngguó.

美   měi   beautiful; pretty

美國	Měiguó	the United States of America	美国
美人	měirén	beautiful woman	美人
美好	měihǎo	beautiful; fine	美好
美女	měinǚ	a beauty	美女
美國人	Měiguórén	American person	美国人

本   běn   origin; foundation; a copy

本人	běnrén	oneself	本人
本日	běnrì	today	本日

本 地	běndì	local area	本 地
本 來	běnlái	originally; at first	本 来
本 土	běntǔ	one's native country	本 土
本 心	běnxīn	one's conscience	本 心
本 子	běnzi	notebook	本 子
一 本	yīběn	a copy	一 本
日 本	Rìběn	Japan	日 本
日 本 人	Rìběnrén	Japanese person	日 本 人
本 地 人	běndìrén	a native person	本 地 人

他是我的美國朋友。
He is my American friend.

他是我的美国朋友。
Tā shì wǒ de Měiguó péngyou.

我也是美國人。
I am also an American.

我也是美国人。
Wǒ yě shì Měiguórén.

今天是美好的日子。
Today is a beautiful day.

今天是美好的日子。
Jīntiān shì měihǎo de rìzi.

她本人沒有來，她朋友來了。
She herself didn't come, but her friend did.

她本人没有来，她朋友来了。
Tā běnrén méiyǒu lái, tā péngyou lái le.

她本來是好人。
She used to be a nice person.

她本来是好人。
Tā běnlái shì hǎorén.

你有沒有本子？
Do you have a notebook?

你有没有本子？
Nǐ yǒu mei yǒu běnzi?

我是日本人，不是中國人。
I am Japanese, not Chinese.

我是日本人，不是中国人。
Wǒ shì Rìběnrén, bú shì Zhōngguórén.

我們都是美國人。
We are all Americans.

我们都是美国人。
Wǒmen dōu shì Měiguórén.

我們都不是美國人。　　　　　　我们都不是美国人。
None of us is American.　　　　　Wǒmen dōu bú shì Měiguórén.

我們不都是美國人。　　　　　　我们 不都是美国人。
Not all of us are Americans.　　　Wǒmen bù dōu shì Měiguórén.

男　　　　　　　nán　　　　male; man; boy; son

男女　　　　nán-nǚ　　　men and women　　　　　　　男女
男人　　　　nánrén　　　man　　　　　　　　　　　　男人
男子　　　　nánzǐ　　　man; male　　　　　　　　　　男子
男家　　　　nánjiā　　　the bridegroom's family　　　男家
男朋友　　　nánpéngyou　boyfriend　　　　　　　　　男朋友

哥　　　　　　　gē　　　　　an elder brother

哥哥　　　　gēge　　　elder brother　　　　　　　　哥哥
大哥　　　　dàgē　　　eldest brother　　　　　　　　大哥

林月明的男朋友是日本人。　　　林月明的男朋友是日本人。
Lin Yueming's boyfriend is　　　Lín Yuèmíng de nánpéngyou shì Rìběnrén.
Japanese.

田大明是美男子。　　　　　　　田大明是美男子。
Tian Daming is a handsome man.　Tián Dàmíng shì měi nánzǐ.

馬國森是她男朋友嗎？　　　　　马国森是她男朋友吗？
Is Ma Guosen her boyfriend?　　Mǎ Guósēn shì tā nánpéngyou ma?

我哥哥是她男朋友。
My elder brother is her boyfriend.

你大哥有女朋友嗎？
Does your eldest brother have a girlfriend?

你大哥有沒有女朋友？
Does your elder brother have a girlfriend?

我哥哥是她男朋友。
Wǒ gēge shì tā nánpéngyou.

你大哥有女朋友吗？
Nǐ dàgē yǒu nǔpéngyou ma?

你大哥有没有女朋友？
Nǐ dàgē yǒu mei yǒu nǔpéngyou?

姐	jié	an elder sister; a general term for young women	
姐姐	jiéjie	elder sister	姐姐
姐夫	jiéfu	elder sister's husband; brother-in-law	姐夫
大姐	dàjié	eldest sister	大姐
小姐	xiǎojié	Miss; young lady	小姐

妹	mèi	younger sister	
妹妹	mèimei	younger sister	妹妹
妹夫	mèifu	younger sister's husband; brother-in-law	妹夫
姐妹	jiémèi	sisters	姐妹

林小姐是我的好朋友。
Miss Lin is my good friend.

她哥哥是我姐夫。
Her elder brother is my brother-in-law (elder sister's husband).

林小姐是我的好朋友。
Lín xiǎojie shì wǒ de hǎo péngyou.

她哥哥是我姐夫。
Tā gēge shì wǒ de jiéfu.

我姐姐也有男朋友。
My elder sister also has a boyfriend.

我姐姐也有男朋友。
Wǒ jiéjie yě yǒu nánpéngyou.

誰是你的妹夫？
Who is your brother-in-law
(younger sister's husband)?

谁是你的妹夫？
Shuí shì nǐ de mèifu?

你是誰的妹妹？
Whose younger sister are you?

你是谁的妹妹？
Nǐ shì shuíde mèimei?

我們是好姐妹。
We are good sisters.

我们是好姐妹。
Wǒmen shì hǎo jiémèi.

我沒有姐姐，也沒有妹妹。
I have neither an elder sister nor a
younger sister.

我没有姐姐，也没有妹妹。
Wǒ méiyǒu jiéjie, yě méiyǒu mèimei.

Exercises Lesson 6

A. Identify the character that is related to each English concept.

1. all, together
    a. 看　　　　b. 早　　　　c. 都　　　　d. 也

2. very, quite
    a. 很　　　　b. 好　　　　c. 的　　　　d. 家

3. each, every
    a. 了　　　　b. 每　　　　c. 母　　　　d. 目

4. light, bright
    a. 們　　　　b. 你　　　　c. 亮　　　　d. 年

5. beautiful
    a. 化　　　　b. 美　　　　c. 石　　　　d. 來

6. who
    a. 誰　　　　b. 同　　　　c. 它　　　　d. 多

7. country
    a. 面　　　　b. 百　　　　c. 國　　　　d. 出

8. foundation
    a. 木　　　　b. 前　　　　c. 地　　　　d. 本

9. elder brother
    a. 姐　　　　b. 平　　　　c. 哥　　　　d. 和

10. younger sister
    a. 明　　　　b. 妹　　　　c. 她　　　　d. 媽

B. Identify the character that is related to each pinyin transcription.

1. guó
    a. 出　　　　b. 國　　　　c. 回　　　　d. 看

2. nán
   a. 男   b. 昨   c. 前   d. 今

3. jié
   a. 回   b. 早   c. 妹   d. 姐

4. hěn
   a. 來   b. 很   c. 好   d. 口

5. měi
   a. 友   b. 尖   c. 在   d. 美

6. běn
   a. 見   b. 本   c. 看   d. 昨

7. gē
   a. 哥   b. 方   c. 每   d. 都

8. shuí
   a. 長   b. 外   c. 誰   d. 在

C. Identify the pinyin transcription that is related to each character.

1. 亮
   a. liàng   b. liāng   c. liáng   d. dáng

2. 都
   a. doū   b. doú   c. dèn   d. dōu

3. 妹
   a. mài   b. mèi   c. màe   d. mēi

4. 國
   a. koū   b. qoū   c. gōn   d. quó

5. 每
   a. měi   b. mēn   c. mèi   d. mūn

6. 男
   a. nān   b. nán   c. nàn   d. wàn

D. Identify the compound word or phrase that is related to each English concept.

1. the moon
   a. 天亮   b. 月光   c. 月亮   d. 明了

2. everybody
   a. 每月   b. 每日   c. 美人   d. 每人

3. all come
   a. 都來   b. 看來   c. 來了   d. 來日

4. whose
   a. 他人   b. 誰的   c. 誰家   d. 誰人

5. country
   a. 國家   b. 我國   c. 國土   d. 天國

6. beauty
   a. 美國   b. 美人   c. 沒人   d. 美好

E. Identify the compound word or phrase that is related to each pinyin transcription.

1. guójīa
   a. 國家   b. 大家   c. 出國   d. 國外

2. měihǎo
   a. 美女   b. 好在   c. 不好   d. 美好

3. běnlái
   a. 日本   b. 本來   c. 沒了   d. 本心

4. nánrén
   a. 家人   b. 男家   c. 男人   d. 每人

5. dàgē
   a. 大哥   b. 大姐   c. 姐夫   d. 小姐

F.   Identify the character that is different in tone from the others.

1.   a. 妹   b. 大   c. 看   d. 哥

2.   a. 男   b. 回   c. 人   d. 都

3.   a. 在   b. 本   c. 小   d. 好

4.   a. 姐   b. 朋   c. 前   d. 來

5.   a. 哥   b. 美   c. 都   d. 家

6.   a. 看   b. 在   c. 妹   d. 前

7.   a. 田   b. 回   c. 國   d. 每

8.   a. 亮   b. 哥   c. 出   d. 山

G.   Fill in the blanks with the appropriate words or phrases.

1.   今晚月亮——很大。
     a. 每每   b. 看來   c. 本來   d. 看看

2.   她——是我女朋友。
     a. 妹妹   b. 哥哥   c. 大人   d. 男人

3.   我明天—日本。
     a. 看   b. 出   c. 很   d. 去

4.   你有沒有外國——？
     a. 國家   b. 國人   c. 朋友   d. 美人

5.   你哥哥是我—朋友。
     a. 每   b. 好   c. 亮   d. 看

6.   我們—是美國人。
     a. 很   b. 好   c. 都   d. 沒

7. 我姐姐 ── 國外。
   a. 看　　　 b. 在　　　 c. 來　　　 d. 每

8. 今晚月亮很 ──── 。
   a. 明了　　 b. 大小　　 c. 明亮　　 d. 看了

H.　Rearrange the word groups to form meaningful sentences.

   1.　美國人，朋友，他的，是 。

   2.　下月，我，中國，去 。

   3.　女朋友，你的，美，很 。

   4.　日本人，是，大家，都，你們 。

   5.　本來，今天，他，來 。

   6.　沒有，大哥，我，女朋友 。

   7.　月亮，大，今晚，很 。

I.　Translate the following into English.

   1.　她每天都很晚回來。

   2.　她的男朋友每天都去看她。

   3.　誰是她的男朋友？

   4.　她沒有哥哥，也沒有妹妹。

   5.　誰是你的大姐？

J.   Translate the following into Chinese.

    1.   She is the wife of my younger brother.

    2.   Who is her ex-husband?

    3.   She goes to see her boyfriend every day.

    4.   She goes out very early every day.

    5.   Are they Chinese?

Answers

A.	B.	C.	D.	E.
1. c	1. b	1. a	1. c	1. a
2. a	2. a	2. d	2. d	2. d
3. b	3. d	3. b	3. a	3. b
4. c	4. b	4. d	4. b	4. c
5. b	5. d	5. a	5. a	5. a
6. a	6. b	6. b	6. b	6. c
7. c	7. a			
8. d	8. c			
9. c				
10. b				

F.	G.	H.
1. d	1. b	1. 他的朋友是美國人。
2. d	2. a	2. 我下月去中國。
3. a	3. d	3. 你的女朋友很美。
4. a	4. c	4. 你們大家都是日本人。
5. b	5. b	5. 他本來今天來。
6. d	6. c	6. 我大哥沒有女朋友。
7. d	7. b	7. 今晚月亮很大。
8. a	8. c	

I.

1. She comes back very late every day.
2. Her boyfriend goes to see her every day.
3. Who is her boyfriend?
4. She doesn't have an elder brother or younger sister.
5. Who is your elder sister?

J.

1. 她是我的弟婦。
2. 誰是她的前夫？
3. 她每天都去看男朋友。
4. 她每天都很早出去。
5. 他們是不是中國人？

第 七 課
Lesson 7

兒 儿   ér   child; baby; son; used as a unit of speech

兒 子	érzi	son; sons	儿 子
兒 女	ér-nǚ	sons and daughters; children	儿 女
小 兒	xiǎo'ér	children; my son	小 儿
女 兒	nǚér	girl; one's daughter	女 儿

說 说   shuō   say; talk; speak

說 好	shuōhǎo	come to an agreement	说 好
說 明	shuōmíng	explain	说 明
說 出	shuōchū	speak out	说 出
小 说	xiǎoshuō	novel; fiction	小 说
好 說	hǎoshuō	thank you for the kind words	好 说
說 不 來	shuōbulái	cannot get along	说 不 来
說 不 上	shuōbushàng	cannot say	说 不 上
小 说 家	xiǎoshuōjiā	novelist	小 说 家
說 不 出 口	shuōbuchūkǒu	unable to utter a word	说 不 出 口
說 不 下 去	shuōbuxiàqù	unable to talk any longer	说 不 下 去

她的兒子在美國。
Her son is in America.

她的儿子在美国。
Tā de érzi zài Měiguó.

大家都説她是美女。
Everybody says that she is a beauty.

大家都说她是美女。
Dàjiā dōu shuō tā shì měinǚ.

我朋友是小説家。
My friend is a novelist.

我朋友是小说家。
Wǒ péngyou shì xiǎoshuōjiā.

我昨天看了一本小説。
I read a novel yesterday.

我昨天看了一本小说。
Wǒ zuótiān kàn le yìběn xiǎoshuō.

我們説好明天去看她。
We agree to go see her tomorrow.

我们说好明天去看她。
Wǒmen shuōhǎo míngtiān qù kàn tā.

我們説不上是好朋友。
I can't say that we are good friends.

我们说不上是好朋友。
Wǒmen shuōbushàng shì hǎo péngyou.

我説明我不是她女兒。
I made it clear that I was not her daughter.

我说明我不是她女儿。
Wǒ shuōmíng wǒ bú shì tā nǚ'ér.

生   shēng   live; grow; be born; life

生 地	shēngdì	uncultivated land	生 地
生 火	shēnghuó	make a fire	生 火
生 前	shēngqián	before one's death	生 前
生 來	shēnglái	since one's birth	生 来
生 人	shēngrén	stranger; living person	生 人
生 日	shēngri	birthday	生 日
生 水	shēngshuǐ	unboiled water	生 水
生 子	shēngzǐ	give birth to a child	生 子
人 生	rénshēng	life	人 生
一 生	yīshēng	a lifetime	一 生

學 学　　xué　　learn; study; imitate

學 好	xuéhǎo	learn good things from others	学 好
學 人	xuérén	scholar	学 人
學 生	xuéshēng	student	学 生
學 説	xuéshuō	theory	学 说
學 友	xuéyǒu	schoolmate	学 友
學 子	xuézǐ	student	学 子
大 學	dàxué	college; university	大 学
中 學	zhōngxué	middle school; high school	中 学
小 學	xiǎoxué	elementary school	小 学
上 學	shàngxué	go to school	上 学

她生前沒有好朋友。
He didn't have any good friends before his death.

她生前没有好朋友。
Tā shēngqián méiyǒu hǎo péngyou.

今天是我的生日。
Today is my birthday.

今天是我的生日。
Jīntiān shì wǒ de shēngri.

她每天一早上學去。
She goes to school early in the morning every day.

她每天一早上学去。
Tā měitiān yīzǎo shàngxué qù.

我是中學生，不是小學生。
I am a high school student, not an elementary school student.

我是中学生，不是小学生。
Wǒ shì zhōngxuésheng, bú shì xiǎoxuésheng.

她是外國學生。
She is a foreign student.

她是外国学生。
Tā shì wàiguóxuésheng.

我不明他的學説。
I don't understand his theory.

我不明他的学说。
Wǒ bù míng tā de xuéshuō.

我好在沒有學他。
I am fortunate that I didn't do what he did.

我好在没有学他。
Wǒ hǎozài méiyǒu xué tā.

他們都是中山大學的學生。
They are all students of Zhongshan University.

他们都是中山大学的学生。
Tāmen dōu shì Zhōngshān dàxué de xuésheng.

弟	dì	younger brother; junior	
弟弟	dìdi	younger brother	弟弟
弟妹	dìmèi	younger brothers and sisters	弟妹
弟婦	dìfù	younger brother's wife	弟妇
弟子	dìzǐ	pupil; disciple	弟子
姐弟	jiědi	elder sister and younger brother	姐弟
小弟	xiǎodi	little brother; little boy	小弟

個 个	gè	a measure word that is placed between a numeral and a noun	
個個	gègè	each and every one	个个
個人	gèrén	individual; oneself	个人
個中	gèzhǒng	within; inside	个中
個子	gèzi	physical size of a person	个子
個兒	gèr (gè+ér)	size; height; stature	个儿
一個	yígè	one; a; an	一个
一個個	yígège	one by one	一个个

我弟弟是美心小學的學生。
My younger brother is a pupil of Meixin Elementary School.

我弟弟是美心小学的学生。
Wǒ dìdi shì Měixīn xiǎoxué de xuésheng.

我弟婦説我弟弟昨晚沒有回家。
My sister-in-law said that my younger brother didn't come home last night.

我弟妇说我弟弟昨晚没有回家。
Wǒ dìfù shuō wǒ dìdi zuówǎn méiyǒu huíjiā.

我妹妹是一個小學生。
My younger sister is an elementary school student.

我妹妹是一个小学生。
Wǒ mèimei shì yígè xiǎoxuésheng.

他們個個都是我朋友。
Each of them is my friend.

他们个个都是我朋友。
Tāmen gègè dōu shì wǒ péngyou.

馬小姐的個子很小。
Miss Ma is very small in stature.

马小姐的个子很小。
Mǎ xiǎojie de gèzi hěn xiǎo.

林大夫有一個兒子，三個女兒。
Dr. Lin has a son and three daughters.

林大夫有一个儿子，三个女儿。
Lín dàifu yǒu yígè érzi, sāngè nǚér

我前天一個人來了日本。
I came alone to Japan the day before yesterday.

我前天一个人来了日本。
Wǒ qiántiān yígè rén lái le Rìběn.

她三個月沒有來我家了。
She hasn't come to my home for three months already.

她三个月没有来我家了。
Tā sāngè yuè méiyǒu lái wǒjiā le.

太   tài   greatest; highest; extremely; a title of respect

太妹	tàimèi	delinquent girl	太妹
太上	tàishàng	the uppermost	太上
太太	tàitai	madame; Mrs.	太太
太晚	tàiwǎn	too late	太晚
太早	tàizǎo	too early	太早
太子	tàizǐ	the crown prince	太子
太夫人	tàifūren	the mother of nobility	太夫人
不太好	bútàihǎo	not very good	不太好

先　　　　　xiān　　　　before; in front; deceased

先 夫	xiānfū	my late husband	先 夫
先 前	xiānqián	before; previously	先 前
先 人	xiānrén	previous generations	先 人
先 生	xiānsheng	Mr.; teacher; husband	先 生
先 天	xiāntiān	innate	先 天
早 先	zǎoxiān	before; some time ago	早 先

牛太太生了沒有？
Has Mrs. Niu delivered already?

牛太太生了没有？
Niú tàitai shēng le méiyǒu?

我回來太晚了。
I came back too late.

我回来太晚了。
Wǒ huílái tàiwǎn le.

馬先生昨天沒有來。
Mr. Ma didn't come yesterday.

马先生昨天没有来。
Mǎ xiānsheng zuótiān méiyǒu lái.

她先生是我的大夫。
Her husband is my doctor.

她先生是我的大夫。
Tā xiānsheng shì wǒ de dàifu.

他是先夫生前的好友。
He was my late husband's good friend.

他是先夫生前的好友。
Tā shì xiānfū xiānqián de hǎo yǒu.

林先生，你好。
Mr. Lin, how do you do?

林先生，你好。
Lín xiānsheng, nǐhǎo?

馬先生，馬太太，你們好嗎？
Mr. Ma, Mrs. Ma, how are you doing?

马先生，马太太，你们好吗？
Mǎ xiānsheng, Mǎ tàitai, nǐmen hǎo ma?

我今天不太好。
I am not very good today.

我今天不太好。
Wǒ jīntiān bú tài hǎo.

父 | fù | father; a male elder

父 子	fùzǐ	father and son	父 子
生 父	shēngfù	biological father	生 父
先 父	xiānfù	my late father	先 父
天 父	tiānfù	Our Heavenly Father	天 父
家 父	jiāfù	my father	家 父

母 | mǔ | mother; female elders

母 國	mǔguó	one's mother country	母 国
母 女	mǔnǚ	mother and daughter	母 女
母 子	mǔzǐ	mother and son	母 子
母 牛	mǔniú	cow	母 牛
父 母	fùmǔ	parents	父 母
家 母	jiāmǔ	my mother	家 母
先 母	xiānmǔ	my late mother	先 母

家父今天不在家。
My father isn't at home today.

家父今天不在家。
Jiāfù jīntiān bú zài jiā.

他的生父不在美國。
His biological father isn't in America.

他的生父不在美国。
Tā de shēngfù bú zài měiguó.

他們父子都在國外。
They, father and son, are out of the country.

他们父子都在国外。
Tāmen fùzǐ dōu zài guówài.

他父母都是我的先生。
His parents are my teachers.

他父母都是我的先生。
Tā fùmǔ dōu shì wǒ de xiānsheng.

他們的母國是日本。
Their mother country is Japan.

他们的母国是日本。
Tāmen de mǔguó shì Rìběn.

什   shén   a component of the interrogative word: 什麼

麼 么   me   a suffix used often in interrogative expression

什麼   shénme   what   什么

你説什麼？
What did you say?

你说什么？
Nǐ shuō shénme?

他是什麼人？
Who is he?

他是什么人？
Tā shì shénme rén?

你的馬是什麼馬？
What kind of horse is yours?

你的马是什么马？
Nǐ de mǎ shì shénme mǎ?

你家中有什麼人？
What other family members do you have?

你家中有什么人？
Nǐ jiāzhōng yǒu shénme rén?

中國有什麼大山？
What are the big mountains in China?

中国有什么大山？
Zhōngguó yǒu shénme dà shān?

今天是什麼好日子？
What special day is today?

今天是什么好日子？
Jīntiān shì shénme hǎorìzi?

我什麼都沒有。
I don't have anything.

我什么都没有？
Wǒ shénme dōu méiyǒu.

Exercises Lesson 7

A. Identify the character that is related to each English phrase or concept.

1. to learn
   a. 第　　　b. 學　　　c. 很　　　d. 都

2. to speak
   a. 説　　　b. 話　　　c. 美　　　d. 看

3. child
   a. 女　　　b. 男　　　c. 兒　　　d. 行

4. greatest
   a. 它　　　b. 少　　　c. 很　　　d. 太

5. before
   a. 晚　　　b. 先　　　c. 姐　　　d. 昨

6. father
   a. 婦　　　b. 妹　　　c. 父　　　d. 夫

7. younger brother
   a. 弟　　　b. 什　　　c. 麼　　　d. 媽

8. to be born
   a. 國　　　b. 生　　　c. 活　　　d. 本

9. mother
   a. 姐　　　b. 年　　　c. 母　　　d. 每

10. a measure word that is placed between a numeral and a noun
    a. 個　　　b. 哥　　　c. 本　　　d. 來

B. Identify the character that is related to each pinyin transcription.

1. tài
   a. 很　　　b. 美　　　c. 太　　　d. 每

2. shuō
   a. 前   b. 昨   c. 唱   d. 説

3. ér
   a. 兒   b. 晚   c. 百   d. 姐

4. mǔ
   a. 本   b. 都   c. 在   d. 母

5. me
   a. 見   b. 友   c. 麼   d. 美

6. xiān
   a. 前   b. 先   c. 看   d. 姐

7. shēng
   a. 生   b. 長   c. 工   d. 外

8. fù
   a. 女   b. 父   c. 大   d. 去

C. Identify the pinyin transcription that is related to each character.

1. 學
   a. sàng   b. xàng   c. xīng   d. xué

2. 弟
   a. dì   b. de   c. dǐ   d. dǔ

3. 個
   a. gà   b. geǐ   c. gè   d. gò

4. 太
   a. tài   b. tā   c. dào   d. dù

5. 什
   a. sēn   b. xīn   c. shén   d. pā

6. 兒
   a. dān   b. tāng   c. de   d. èr

D. Identify the compound word or phrase that is related to each English concept.

    1.   novel
        a. 小兒   b. 小說   c. 好說   d. 說明

    2.   daughter
        a. 女兒   b. 婦女   c. 美女   d. 女人

    3.   before one's death
        a. 前生   b. 看來   c. 生來   d. 生前

    4.   a theory
        a. 學子   b. 說明   c. 學說   d. 大學

    5.   younger brother
        a. 姐姐   b. 弟弟   c. 哥哥   d. 個個

    6.   too late
        a. 太上   b. 太子   c. 太晚   d. 太早

E. Identify the compound word or phrase that is related to each pinyin transcription.

    1.   xiānsheng
        a. 人生   b. 早先   c. 先生   d. 先人

    2.   fùmǔ
        a. 婦人   b. 父母   c. 父子   d. 夫婦

    3.   shuōchū
        a. 說出   b. 出來   c. 出去   d. 說明

    4.   shēngrén
        a. 家人   b. 生人   c. 好人   d. 美人

    5.   dàxué
        a. 大學   b. 大姐   c. 小學   d. 學友

    6.   tàitai
        a. 弟弟   b. 太太   c. 個個   d. 每每

F.   Identify the character that is different in tone from the others.

1.   a. 前   b. 人   c. 學   d. 説

2.   a. 出   b. 太   c. 生   d. 都

3.   a. 在   b. 大   c. 兒   d. 目

4.   a. 國   b. 母   c. 前   d. 來

5.   a. 好   b. 美   c. 先   d. 母

6.   a. 弟   b. 什   c. 妹   d. 父

7.   a. 田   b. 回   c. 兒   d. 説

8.   a. 麼   b. 了   c. 的   d. 學

G.   Fill in the blanks with the appropriate words or phrases.

1.   大家 —— 她是美女。
      a. 明明   b. 小説   c. 都説   d. 看看

2.   今天是我女朋友的 ——。
      a. 生日   b. 哥哥   c. 小兒   d. 生子

3.   明天是 — 的生日?
      a. 本   b. 個   c. 每   d. 誰

4.   你朋友是——人?
      a. 兒女   b. 上山   c. 什麼   d. 沒有

5.   我弟弟是 —— 小學生。
      a. 每個   b. 一個   c. 每每   d. 説出

6.   他的 —— 是日本人。
      a. 先生   b. 人生   c. 生前   d. 生火

7. 馬太太 ━ 了 一 個 女 兒 。
    a. 說　　　b. 在　　　c. 生　　　d. 先

8. 他 的 ━━ 很 大 。
    a. 學 說　　b. 個 子　　c. 一 生　　d. 日 子

H. Translate the following into English.

1. 她 的 兒 子 是 我 姐 姐 的 學 生 。

2. 你 說 什 麼 ？

3. 誰 是 林 先 生 ？

4. 你 的 父 母 是 不 是 在 美 國 ？

5. 你 有 什 麼 小 說 ？

I. Translate the following into Chinese.

1. I have three younger brothers.

2. His wife is an American.

3. I made it clear that I didn't have his novel.

4. He is a good student.

5. Is she a college student?

Answers

A.	B.	C.	D.	E.
1. b	1. c	1. d	1. b	1. c
2. a	2. d	2. a	2. a	2. b
3. c	3. a	3. c	3. d	3. a
4. d	4. d	4. a	4. c	4. b
5. b	5. c	5. c	5. b	5. a
6. c	6. b	6. d	6. c	6. b
7. a	7. a			
8. b	8. b			
9. c				
10. a				

F.	G.
1. d	1. c
2. b	2. a
3. c	3. d
4. b	4. c
5. c	5. b
6. b	6. a
7. d	7. c
8. d	8. b

H.

1. Her son is my elder sister's student.
2. What did you say?
3. Who is Mr. Lin?
4. Are your parents in the United States?
5. What kind of novels do you have?

I.

1. 我有三個弟弟。
2. 他的太太是美國人。
3. 我說明我沒有他的小說。
4. 他是一個好學生。
5. 她是一個大學生嗎？

第八課
Lesson 8

會 会　huì　　will; shall; to meet; meeting; party; to be able to

會 說	huìshuō	able to talk eloquently	会 说
會 心	huìxīn	feel the same way	会 心
會 兒	huìr (huì + ér)	a moment	会 儿
不 會	búhuì	will not; unable to	不 会
生 日 會	shēngrihuì	birthday party	生 日 会
學 生 會	xuéshēnghuì	student association	学 生 会
一 會 兒	yīhuìr	a little while	一 会 儿

定　　dìng　　decide; to fix; settle; certainly

定 本	dìngběn	the finalized version of a book	定 本
定 心	dìngxīn	feel calm	定 心
一 定	yídìng	certainly; definitely	一 定
不 一 定	bùyídìng	uncertain; not sure	不 一 定

她會不會來？
Will she come?

她会不会来？
Tā huì bu huì lái?

你會來我的生日會嗎？
Will you come to my birthday party?

你会来我的生日会吗？
Nǐ huì lái wǒ de shēngrihuì ma?

她明天會來看我。
She will come to see me tomorrow.

她明天会来看我。
Tā míngtiān huì lái kàn wǒ.

我出去一會兒。
I am going out for a little while.

我出去一会儿。
Wǒ chūqu yīhuìr.

看來明天會下雨。
It looks like it will rain tomorrow.

看来明天会下雨。
Kànlái míngtiān huì xià yǔ.

我今天晚上不會回來。
I will not come back tonight.

我今天晚上不会回来。
Wǒ jīntiān wǎnshang bú huì huílai.

你們大學有沒有中國學生會？
Is there a Chinese student association at your university?

你们大学有没有中国学生会？
Nǐmen dàxué yǒu mei yǒu Zhōngguó xuéshenghuì?

我明天一定會來看你。
I will definitely come to see you tomorrow.

我明天一定会来看你。
Wǒ míngtiān yídìng huì lái kàn nǐ.

他不一定會來。
He may or may not come.

他不一定会来。
Tā bú yídìng huì lái.

這 这　　zhè　　this

這麼	zhème	such; so	这么
這個	zhège	this one; this	这个
這兒	zhèr (zhè + èr)	here	这儿
這一回	zhèyìhuí	this time	这一回
這麼一來	zhèmeyìlái	as a result	这么一来

書 书   shū   book

書 本	shūběn	book	书 本
書 目	shūmù	booklist; book catalog	书 目
書 生	shūshēng	student; scholar	书 生
看 書	kànshū	read a book	看 书
四 書	sìshū	The Four Books	四 书

這是什麼？
What is this?

这是什么？
Zhè shì shénme?

這是本子。
This is a notebook.

这是本子。
Zhè shì běnzi.

她是這麼美！
She is so beautiful!

她是这么美！
Tā shì zhème měi!

今晚的月亮是這麼大！
The moon is so big tonight!

今晚的月亮是这么大！
Jīnwǎn de yuèliang shì zhème dà!

這個月我沒有去日本。
I didn't go to Japan this month.

这个月我没有去日本。
Zhège yuè wǒ méiyǒu qù Rìběn.

你在看什麼書？
What book are you reading?

你在看什么书？
Nǐ zài kàn shénme shū?

這本書好看嗎？
Is this book interesting to read?

这本书好看吗？
Zhè běn shū hǎo kàn ma?

這是一本美國小說。
This is an American novel.

这是一本美国小说。
Zhè shì yì běn Měiguó xiǎoshuō.

這三本書是誰的？
Who owns these three books?

这三本书是谁的？
Zhè sān běn shū shì shuí de?

那	nà	that	
那 個	nàge	that one	那 个
那 麼	nàme	like that; so; then; in that way	那 么
那 兒	nàr (nà + ér)	that time; then	那 儿
那 天	nàtiān	that day	那 天

哪	nǎ (něi)	which; what	
哪 個	nǎge	which	哪 个
哪 兒	nǎr (nǎ + ér)	where	哪 儿

文	wén	composition; language; a surname	
文 火	wénhuǒ	low heat (in cooking)	文 火
文 明	wénmíng	civilization	文 明
文 人	wénrén	a man of letters	文 人
文 書	wénshū	documents	文 书
文 學	wénxué	literature	文 学
天 文	tiānwén	astronomy	天 文
中 文	zhōngwén	Chinese language	中 文
外 文	wàiwén	foreign language	外 文
日 文	rìwén	Japanese language	日 文
文 學 家	wénxuéjiā	a literate man	文 学 家
天 文 學	tiānwénxué	astronomy	天 文 学

那是誰？
Who is that?

那是谁？
Nà shì shuí (shéi)?

那是我大姐。
That is my eldest sister.

那是我大姐。
Nà shì wǒ dàjiě.

她那天有沒有來？
Did she come that day?

她那天有没有来？
Tā nàtiān yǒu mei yǒu lái?

你有沒有中文書？
Do you have any Chinese language books?

你有没有中文书？
Nǐ yǒu mei yǒu zhōngwén shū?

我有五本中文書。
I have five Chinese language books.

我有五本中文书。
Wǒ yǒu wǔběn zhōngwén shū.

文先生是本地的一個文學家。
Mr. Wen is a local literate person.

文先生是本地的一个文学家。
Wén xiānsheng shì běndì de yígè wénxuéjiā.

你會看日文嗎？
Can you read Japanese?

你会看日文吗？
Nǐ huì kàn rìwén ma?

你的中文好嗎？
Is your Chinese good?

你的中文好吗？
Nǐ de zhōngwén hǎo ma?

你的中文先生是誰？
Who is your Chinese language teacher?

你的中文先生是谁？
Nǐ de zhōngwén xiānsheng shì shuí?

方	fāng	square; method; direction; just now; a surname	
方的	fāngde	square in shape	方的
方子	fāngzi	medical prescription	方子
地方	dìfang	place; space; aspect	地方
大方	dàfang	poised; natural	大方

校 xiào school

校門	xiàomén	the gate of a school or college	校门
校外	xiàowài	outside the school or college	校外
校友	xiàoyǒu	an alumnus	校友
學校	xuéxiào	school	学校
校友會	xiàoyǒuhuì	an alumni association	校友会

這是什麼地方？
What place is this?

这是什么地方？
Zhè shì shénme dìfang?

他是什麼地方人？
Where is he from?
(*lit.* He is what place person?)

他是什么地方人？
Tā shì shénme dìfang rén?

方文美很美，是不是？
Fang Wenwei is very beautiful, isn't she?

方文美很美，是不是？
Fāng Wénměi hěn měi, shì bu shì?

方文美很美，也很大方。
Fang Wenwei is very beautiful; she is
also very poised.

方文美很美，也很大方。
Fāng Wénměi hěn měi, yě hěn dàfang.

你去什麼地方？
Where are you going?

你去什么地方？
Nǐ qù shénme dìfang?

你是什麼學校的學生？
Of what school are you a student?

你是什么学校的学生？
Nǐ shì shénme xuéxiào de xuésheng?

我是美國大學的學生。
I am a student of American University.

我是美国大学的学生。
Wǒ shì Měiguó dàxué de xuésheng.

我學校有五十個外國學生。
There are fifty foreign students in my school.

我学校有五十个外国学生。
Wǒ xuéxiào yǒu wǔshì gè wàiguó
xuésheng.

多 duō many; much; more

多 大	duōdà	How big? How old?	多 大
多 多	duōduō	a great deal	多 多
多 方	duōfāng	in many ways	多 方
多 好	duōhǎo	How nice!	多 好
多 麼	duōme	how; what	多 么
多 美	duōměi	how beautiful	多 美
多 心	duōxīn	suspicious	多 心
好 多	hǎoduō	a lot of; a good many	好 多
很 多	hěnduō	very much; many	很 多

過 过 guò pass; across; past; mistake; spend (time)

過 多	guòduō	too many; too much	过 多
過 來	guòlái	come over	过 来
過 門	guòmén	to pass the door; to get married (for a girl)	过 门
過 去	guòqù	in the past; to pass	过 去
過 目	guòmù	take a look	过 目
過 人	guòrén	surpass others	过 人
過 火	guòhuǒ	go too far	过 火
不 過	búguò	but; merely; however	不 过
大 過	dàguò	a serious mistake	大 过
過 不 去	guòbuqù	cannot get through; feel sorry for	过 不 去

中國有很多人口。
China has a huge population.

中国有很多人口。
Zhōngguó yǒu hénduō rénkǒu.

中國的山川多美！
China's landscape is so beautiful!

中国的山川多美！
Zhōngguò de shānchuān duōměi !

美國的女人是多麼大方！
American women are so poised!

美国的女人是多么大方！
Měiguò de nǔrén shì duōme dàfang!

方太太是一個多心的女人。
Mrs. Fang is a very suspicious woman.

方太太是一个多心的女人。
Fāng tàitai shì yígè duōxīn de nǔrén.

你學校多大？
How big is your school?

你学校多大？
Nǐ xuéxiào duōdà?

你去過中國沒有？
Have you been to China?

你去过中国没有？
Nǐ qù guo Zhōngguó méiyou?

我沒有去過中國，不過我去
過日本。
I have never been to China, but I have
been to Japan.

我没有去过中国，不过我去
过日本。
Wǒ méiyǒu qù guo Zhōngguó, búguò wǒ
qù guo Rìběn.

你有沒有學過日文？
Have you ever studied Japanese?

你有没有学过日文？
Nǐ yǒu mei yǒu xué guo Rìwén?

那本書你看過嗎？
Have you ever read that book?

那本书你看过吗？
Nà běn shū nǐ kàn guo ma?

他有很多過人的地方。
He surpasses others in many ways.

他有很多过人的地方。
Tā yǒu hěnduō guòrén de dìfang.

年   nián   year; age; annual

年會	niánhuì	an annual meeting	年会
年年	niánnián	year after year	年年
年月	niányue	times; age	年月
今年	jīnnián	this year	今年
明年	míngnián	next year	明年
去年	qùnián	last year	去年
前年	qiánnián	the year before last	前年
每年	měinián	every year	每年
天年	tiánnián	natural life span	天年
過年	guònián	pass the new year	过年

海   hǎi   sea; ocean

海口	hǎikǒu	seaport	海口
海馬	hǎimǎ	sea horse	海马
海水	hǎishuǐ	seawater	海水
海外	hǎiwài	overseas; abroad	海外
大海	dàhǎi	the ocean	大海
人海	rénhǎi	a sea of people	人海
學海	xuéhǎi	a sea of learning	学海
上海	shànghǎi	Shanghai	上海
出海	chūhǎi	go to sea	出海

你今年多大？
How old are you (this year)?

你今年多大？
Nǐ jīnnián duō dà?

我今年二十一。
I am twenty-one (this year).

我今年二十一。
Wǒ jīnnián èrshí yī.

你年年都去日本嗎？
Do you go to Japan every year?

你年年都去日本吗？
Nǐ niánnián dōu qù Rìběn ma?

我每年都去日本。
I go to Japan every year.

我每年都去日本。
Wǒ měinián dōu qù Rìběn.

前年是什麼年？
What year was the year before last?

前年是什么年？
Qiánnián shì shénme nián?

前年是一九九七年。
The year before last was 1997.

前年是一九九七年。
Qiánnián shì yījiǔjiǔqī nián.

海外的中國人很多。
There are many Chinese people overseas.

海外的中国人很多。
Hǎiwài de Zhōngguó rén hěn duō.

美國有什麼海口？
What are some of the seaports in the United States?

美国有什么海口？
Měiguó yǒu shénme hǎikǒu?

他們每天一早出海。
They go to the sea in the early morning every day.

他们每天一早出海。
Tāmen měitiān yīzǎo chū hǎi.

我明年會去上海學中文。
I will go to Shanghai next year to study the Chinese language.

我明年会去上海学中文。
Wǒ míngnián huì qù Shànghǎi xué Zhōngwén.

在上海的外國人很多都會
看中文。
Many foreigners in Shanghai can read Chinese.

在上海的外国人很多都会
看中文。
Zài Shànghǎi de wàiguórén hěn duō dōu huì kàn Zhōngwén.

Exercises Lesson 8

A.   Identify the character that is related to the English word(s) or phrase(s).

1.   sea
   a. 説   b. 江   c. 河   d. 海

2.   direction, square
   a. 方   b. 力   c. 都   d. 尖

3.   year, age
   a. 本   b. 年   c. 來   d. 森

4.   many, much
   a. 可   b. 會   c. 多   d. 都

5.   school
   a. 生   b. 校   c. 長   d. 城

6.   across, past
   a. 過   b. 國   c. 近   d. 遠

7.   to decide, to calm
   a. 長   b. 家   c. 什   d. 定

8.   this
   a. 兒   b. 這   c. 麼   d. 那

9.   book
   a. 見   b. 會   c. 書   d. 畫

10.   language
   a. 夫   b. 它   c. 本   d. 文

B.   Identify the character that is related to each pinyin transcription.

1.   nà
   a. 都   b. 兒   c. 那   d. 個

2. duō
a. 多   b. 中   c. 國   d. 母

3. wén
a. 沒   b. 文   c. 本   d. 人

4. huì
a. 回   b. 很   c. 會   d. 在

5. zhè
a. 這   b. 是   c. 哥   d. 目

6. fāng
a. 每   b. 方   c. 馬   d. 美

7. guò, guo
a. 學   b. 都   c. 過   d. 外

8. nián
a. 婦   b. 年   c. 弟   d. 哥

C. Identify the pinyin transcription that is related to each character.

1. 書
a. shūn   b. shū   c. xīn   d. shuō

2. 定
a. dìng   b. dōng   c. tōng   d. pīn

3. 海
a. kǎi   b. hěn   c. hǎi   d. kōn

4. 校
a. xiào   b. hù   c. hǎo   d. huǒ

5. 文
a. wěn   b. wǐn   c. wán   d. wén

6. 那
a. nà   b. ná   c. nén   d. nīng

D. Identify the compound word or phrase that is related to each English concept.

1. definitely
    a. 一會   b. 一定   c. 不會   d. 一個

2. overseas
    a. 海外   b. 外國   c. 生前   d. 大海

3. to read a book
    a. 四書   b. 看來   c. 看書   d. 書目

4. Chinese language
    a. 文學   b. 中文   c. 中外   d. 中學

5. last year
    a. 前年   b. 去年   c. 今年   d. 明年

6. poised and natural
    a. 大方   b. 大夫   c. 太好   d. 友好

E. Identify the compound word or phrase that is related to each pinyin transcription.

1. búguò
    a. 美國   b. 不過   c. 不會   d. 來過

2. huìr
    a. 會兒   b. 小兒   c. 這兒   d. 會心

3. shūběn
    a. 看出   b. 書本   c. 一本   d. 日本

4. dìfang
    a. 地上   b. 大方   c. 地方   d. 大地

5. xuéxiào
    a. 大學   b. 學校   c. 校友   d. 學友

6. duōme
    a. 這麼   b. 什麼   c. 多麼   d. 那麼

F. Identify the character that is different in tone from the others.

1.   a. 過   b. 下   c. 地   d. 本

2.   a. 那   b. 方   c. 生   d. 中

3.   a. 好   b. 美   c. 校   d. 小

4.   a. 人   b. 多   c. 文   d. 來

5.   a. 這   b. 那   c. 會   d. 年

6.   a. 大   b. 海   c. 妹   d. 上

7.   a. 定   b. 說   c. 方   d. 都

8.   a. 這   b. 書   c. 過   d. 定

G. Fill in the blanks with the appropriate words or phrases.

1.   我 明 天 —— 會 去 學 校 。
        a. 來過   b. 一定   c. 一會   d. 什麼

2.   他 的 女 朋 友 很 ——。
        a. 大方   b. 美人   c. 好友   d. 不會

3.   她 有 —— 好 朋 友 。
        a. 這麼   b. 很多   c. 每個   d. 不是

4.   他 沒 有 —— 中 國 。
        a. 看看   b. 學過   c. 什麼   d. 去過

5.   她 姐 姐 是 —— 美 !
        a. 多麼   b. 很好   c. 每每   d. 什麼

6.   你 學 校 在 什 麼 —— ? 。
        a. 學說   b. 地上   c. 沒有   d. 地方

7. 那是 —— 中文書。
   a. 一定　　b. 一本　　c. 一個　　d. 一家

8. 這是 —— 書？
   a. 本子　　b. 什麼　　c. 那麼　　d. 多麼

H. Rearrange the word groups to form meaningful sentences.

1. 學過，你，嗎，中文？

2. 上海人，我，是，朋友。

3. 一定，他們，日本人，是。

4. 書，這本，我的，不是。

5. 那個，沒有，人，子女。

6. 她，中文，學，去上海。

7. 學校，我，學生，有很多。

I. Translate the following into English.

1. 我沒有看過那本書。

2. 那個人一定不是好人。

3. 他的中文很好。

4. 他們明年會來美國。

5. 今晚我在家看書。

J. Translate the following into Chinese.

    1.   What is that?

    2.   Where is your horse?

    3.   Have you ever read that book?

    4.   Can you read that Chinese book?

    5.   Are there foreign students in your school?

Answers

A.	B.	C.	D.	E.
1. d	1. c	1. b	1. b	1. b
2. a	2. a	2. a	2. a	2. a
3. b	3. b	3. c	3. c	3. b
4. c	4. c	4. a	4. b	4. c
5. b	5. a	5. d	5. b	5. b
6. a	6. b	6. a	6. a	6. c
7. d	7. c			
8. b	8. b			
9. c				
10. d				

F.	G.	H.
1. d	1. b	1. 你學過中文嗎？
2. a	2. a	2. 我朋友是上海人。
3. c	3. b	3. 他們一定是日本人。
4. b	4. d	4. 這本書不是我的。
5. d	5. a	5. 那個人沒有子女。
6. b	6. d	6. 她去上海學中文。
7. a	7. b	7. 我學校有很多學生。
8. b	8. b	

I.

1. I have not read that book.
2. That guy is definitely not a good person.
3. His Chinese language is very good.
4. They will come to the United States next year.
5. I am going to stay home to read a book tonight.

J.

1. 那是什麼？
2. 你的馬在那兒？
3. 你看過那本書嗎？
4. 你會看那本中文書嗎？
5. 你的學校有外國學生嗎？

第九課

Lesson 9

星　xīng　star; a movie star

星 火	xīnghuǒ	spark	星 火	
星 星	xīngxīng	stars; tiny spots	星 星	
明 星	míngxīng	movie star	明 星	
火 星	huǒxīng	Mars	火 星	
水 星	shuǐxīng	Mercury	水 星	
木 星	mùxīng	Jupiter	木 星	
土 星	tǔxīng	Saturn	土 星	

期　qī　a period of time; hope; expect

星 期	xīngqī	week	星 期	
日 期	rìqī	date	日 期	
學 期	xuéqī	school term	学 期	
定 期	dìngqī	arrange a date	定 期	
過 期	guòqī	exceed the time limit; overdue	过 期	
星 期 日	xīngqīrì	Sunday	星 期 日
星 期 一	xīngqīyī	Monday	星 期 一
星 期 二	xīngqīèr	Tuesday	星 期 二
星 期 三	xīngqīsān	Wednesday	星 期 三
星 期 四	xīngqīsì	Thursday	星 期 四
星 期 五	xīngqīwǔ	Friday	星 期 五
星 期 六	xīngqīliù	Saturday	星 期 六

121

她是我國的大明星。
She is a great movie star in my country.

她是我国的大明星。
Tā shì wǒ guó de dà míngxīng.

她在門外看星星。
She is outside looking at the stars.

她在门外看星星。
Tā zài ménwài kàn xīngxīng.

天上有很多星星。
There are many stars in the sky.

天上有很多星星。
Tiānshàng yǒu hěn duō xīngxīng.

誰説她是明星？
Who says that she is a movie star?

谁说她是明星？
Shuí (shéi) shuō tā shì míngxīng?

那不是火星，那是土星。
That is not Mars, that is Saturn.

那不是火星，那是土星。
Nà bú shì huǒxīng, nà shì tǔxīng.

今天是星期一。
Today is Monday.

今天是星期一。
Jīntiān shì xīngqīyī.

他去日本的日期定了沒有？
Has he set a date for his trip to Japan?

他去日本的日期定了没有？
Tā qù Rìběn de rìqī dìng le měiyou?

那本書有沒有過期？
Is that book overdue?

那本书有没有过期？
Nà běn shū yǒu mei yǒu guòqī?

我這學期在家學中文。
I am studying Chinese at home this
school term.

我这学期在家学中文。
Wǒ zhè xuéqī zài jiā xué zhōngwén.

她下星期去學中文。
She is going to study Chinese next week.

她下星期去学中文。
Tā xià xīngqī qù xué zhōngwén.

爸　　　　bà　　　　father; dad

爸爸　　　bàba　　　father; papa　　　　　　　　　爸爸

見 见　　jiàn　　see; receive (visitors, etc.)

見 地	jiàndì	insight; views; ideas	见 地	
見 方	jiànfāng	square	见 方	
見 過	jiànguò	have seen	见 过	
見 人	jiànrén	meet people	见 人	
見 外	jiànwài	treat as a stranger	见 外	
看 見	kànjiàn	see; catch sight of	看 见	
不 見	bújiàn	to not see	不 见	
會 見	huìjiàn	to meet with	会 见	
見 天 日	jiàntiānrì	see justice done	见 天 日	

我爸爸在國外。
My father is out of the country.

我爸爸在国外。
Wǒ bàba zài guówài.

她爸爸一個星期沒有回家了。
Her father hasn't come home for a week.

她爸爸一个星期没有回家了。
Tā bàba yīge xīngqī méiyǒu huíjiā le.

他爸爸是一個好好先生。
His father is a nice guy.

他爸爸是一个好好先生。
Tā bàba shì yīge hǎohǎo xiānsheng.

有人說她爸爸不是他的生父。
Somebody says that her father is not her biological father.

有人说她爸爸不是他的生父。
Yǒurén shuō tā bàba bú shì tā de shēngfù.

你有沒有見過水牛。
Have you ever seen a water buffalo?

你有没有见过水牛。
Nǐ yǒu mei yǒu jiànguò shuǐniú?

你太見外了。
Don't treat yourself like a stranger here.

你太见外了。
Nǐ tài jiànwài le.

我的書不見了。
My book has disappeared.

我的书不见了。
Wǒ de shū bújiàn le.

你看見方小姐了嗎？
Have you seen Miss Fang?

你看见方小姐了吗？
Nǐ kànjiàn Fāng xiǎojie le ma?

我在上海看見田大夫。
I saw Dr. Tian in Shanghai.

我在上海看见田大夫。
Wǒ zài Shànghǎi kànjiàn Tián dàifu.

今天我看見很多馬。
I saw many horses today.

今天我看见很多马。
Jīntiān wǒ kànjiàn hěn duō mǎ.

媽 妈　　　mā　　　　mother; mom

媽媽　　māma　　　mama; mother　　　　　妈妈

和　　　　hé　　　　and; harmony; peace

和好	héhǎo	maintain friendly relations	和好
和會	héhuì	peace conference	和会
不和	bùhé	to not get along well	不和
説和	shuōhé	to mediate a settlement	说和

我媽媽是一個好太太。
My mother is a good wife.

我妈妈是一个好太太。
Wǒ māma shì yīge hǎo tàitai.

我媽媽是我爸爸的學生。
My mother was my father's student.

我妈妈是我爸爸的学生。
Wǒ māma shì wǒ bàba de xuésheng.

媽媽，你有沒有看見我的書？
Mama, have you seen my book?

妈妈，你有没有看见我的书？
Māma, nǐ yǒu mei yǒu kànjian wǒ de shū?

媽媽說過他不會來。
Mama said that he won't come.

妈妈说过他不会来。
Māma shuō guo tā bú huì lái.

她們姐妹不和。
The sisters do not get along with each other.

她们姐妹不和。
Tāmen jiémèi bù hé.

他們和好了嗎？
Have they made up now?

他们和好了吗？
Tāmen héhǎo le ma?

他們有一個兒子和三個女兒。
They have a son and three daughters.

他们有一个儿子和三个女儿。
Tāmen yǒu yīge érzi hé sānge nǚer.

這個學期我在家學中文和日文。
This school term I am staying home to study Chinese and Japanese.

这个学期我在家学中文和日文。
Zhège xuéqī wǒ zài jiā xué zhōngwén hé rìwén.

言　　　　yán　　　words; say; speech; language

言 和	yánhé	to become reconciled	言 和
言 明	yánmíng	to make it clear; to state clearly	言 明
大 言	dàyán	boasting	大 言
文 言	wényán	classical Chinese	文 言
多 言	duōyán	loquacious; very talkative	多 言
方 言	fāngyán	dialect	方 言
口 出 大 言	kǒuchūdàyán	brag; boast	口 出 大 言
有 言 在 先	yǒuyánzàixiān	to have made the promise beforehand; to forewarn; to make clear beforehand	有 言 在 先

語 语　yǔ　language; words; speech

語 言	yǔyán	speech; language	语 言
語 文	yǔwén	language and literature	语 文
口 語	kǒuyǔ	spoken language	口 语
土 語	tǔyǔ	dialect	土 语
言 語	yányǔ	language; words	言 语
外 語	wàiyǔ	foreign language	外 语
外 來 語	wàiláiyǔ	words of foreign origin	外 来 语
語 言 學	yǔyánxué	linguistics	语 言 学
不 言 不 語	bùyánbùyǔ	to utter not a single word	不 言 不 语
言 三 語 四	yánsānyǔsì	to criticize without much thinking	言 三 语 四

她是一個多言的女人。
She is a very talkative woman.

她是一个多言的女人。
Tā shì yīge duōyán de nǚrén.

文大川是個口出大言的人。
Wen Dachuan is one who likes to brag about his success.

文大川是个口出大言的人。
Wén Dàchuān shì ge kǒuchūdàyán de rén.

我有言在先，我一定會去。
To keep my word, I will definitely go.

我有言在先，我一定会去。
Wǒ yǒu yán zài xiān, wǒ yídìng huì qù.

我有一本文言小说。
I have a novel written in classical Chinese.

我有一本文言小说。
Wǒ yǒu yìběn wényán xiǎoshuō.

我的國文先生也是語言學家。
My Chinese language teacher is also a linguist.

我的国文先生也是语言学家。
Wǒ de guówén xiānsheng yě shì yǔyánxuéjiā.

我有一本中文的語言學書。
I have a Chinese book on the subject of linguistics.

我有一本中文的语言学书。
Wǒ yǒu yìběn zhōngwén de yǔyánxué shū.

她來日本的目的是學日本語言。
The purpose of her coming to Japan is to study Japanese.

她来日本的目的是学日本语言。
Tā lái Rìběn de mùdì shì xué Rìběn yǔyán.

身　　shēn　　body; trunk; oneself

身家	shēnjiā	family background	身家
身上	shēnshang	on one's body	身上
身心	shēnxīn	body and mind	身心
身子	shēnzi	body; trunk	身子
上身	shàngshēn	upper body	上身
下身	xiàshēn	lower body	下身
人身	rénshēn	human body	人身
出身	chūshēn	personal background	出身
本身	běnshēn	in itself	本身
前身	qiánshēn	predecessor	前身

孕　　yùn　　to be pregnant; to conceive

孕婦	yùnfù	pregnant woman	孕妇
孕期	yùnqī	gestation; period of time for pregnancy	孕期
身孕	shēnyùn	pregnancy	身孕

127

他的身家很好。
His family background is very good.

他的身家很好。
Tā de shēnjiā hěn hǎo.

小心你的身子。
Take care of your body.

小心你的身子。
Xiǎoxīn nǐ de shēnzi.

中美大學的前身是美國中學。
Chinese-American University's predecessor was the former American High School.

中美大学的前身是美国中学。
Zhōngměi dàxué de qiánshēn shì Měiguó zhōngxué.

他身心都很好。
His body and mind are in good shape.

他身心都很好。
Tā shēnxīn dōu hěn hǎo.

他出身好。
He has a good personal background.

他出身好。
Tā chūshēn hǎo.

馬太太有了三個月的身孕。
Mrs. Ma has been pregnant for three months.

马太太有了三个月的身孕。
Mǎ tàitai yǒu le sānge yuè de shēnyùn.

那個孕婦是誰的太太。
Whose wife is that pregnant woman?

那个孕妇是谁的太太。
Nà ge yùnfù shì shuí (shéi) de tàitai.

孕期是九個月。
The period of pregnancy is nine months.

孕期是九个月。
Yùnqī shì jiǔge yuè.

方太太看來有身孕。
It looks like Mrs. Fang is pregnant.

方太太看来有身孕。
Fāng tàitai kànlái yǒu shēnyùn.

久　　　　jǐu　　　　longtime; lasting

久 久	jǐujǐu	for a long time; longtime	久 久
不 久	bùjǐu	before long; soon after	不 久
日 久	rìjǐu	when time has passed	日 久
很 久	hěnjǐu	very long time	很 久

謝 謝　　xiè　　thank; a surname

謝 謝	xièxiè	thank you; thanks	谢 谢
不 謝	búxiè	no need to thank (you're welcome)	不 谢
多 謝	duōxiè	thanks a lot	多 谢
謝 天 謝 地	xiètiān-xièdì	thank goodness; thank Heaven	谢 天 谢 地

她久久不出來。
She still has not come out for a long time.

她久久不出来。
Tā jiǔjiǔ bù chūlai.

日久見人心。
Time will reveal one's true nature.

日久见人心。
Rìjiǔ jiàn rénxīn.

我很久沒看見他了。
I haven't seen him for a long time.

我很久没看见他了。
Wǒ hěnjiǔ méi kànjian tā le.

你好嗎？
How are you?

你好吗？
Nǐ hǎo ma?

我很好，謝謝你。你也好嗎？
I am very well, thank you.
How about you?

我很好，谢谢你。你也好吗？
Wǒ hěn hǎo, xièxie nǐ. Nǐ yě hǎo ma?

我也好，謝謝。
I am fine too, thank you.

我也好，谢谢。
Wǒ yě hǎo, xièxie.

大家都説你太太有身孕了，
是嗎？
Everybody says that your wife is pregnant,
is it true?

大家都说你太太有身孕了，
是吗？
Dàjiā dōu shuō nǐ tàitai yǒu shēnyùn le,
shì ma?

是的，謝天謝地！
Yes. Thank goodness!

是的，谢天谢地！
Shì de, xiètiān-xièdì!

Exercises Lesson 9

A. Identify the character that is related to each English word or phrase.

1. father
    a. 嗎　　　b. 高　　　c. 爸　　　d. 空

2. star
    a. 期　　　b. 望　　　c. 表　　　d. 星

3. pregnant
    a. 孕　　　b. 里　　　c. 兩　　　d. 多

4. word
    a. 力　　　b. 言　　　c. 方　　　d. 向

5. mother
    a. 姐　　　b. 婦　　　c. 父　　　d. 媽

6. and
    a. 平　　　b. 和　　　c. 近　　　d. 多

7. body
    a. 高　　　b. 面　　　c. 身　　　d. 什

8. to thank
    a. 書　　　b. 要　　　c. 敏　　　d. 謝

9. longtime
    a. 個　　　b. 計　　　c. 久　　　d. 可

10. speech
    a. 主　　　b. 由　　　c. 語　　　d. 信

B. Identify the character that is related to each pinyin transcription.

1. jiǔ
    a. 四　　　b. 文　　　c. 多　　　d. 久

2. yǔ
   a. 語   b. 會   c. 見   d. 方

3. qī
   a. 期   b. 星   c. 來   d. 很

4. bà
   a. 這   b. 爸   c. 哥   d. 方

5. yán
   a. 言   b. 過   c. 外   d. 都

6. mā
   a. 學   b. 回   c. 媽   d. 弟

7. xiè
   a. 家   b. 每   c. 是   d. 謝

8. shēn
   a. 孕   b. 個   c. 身   d. 年

C. Identify the pinyin transcription that is related to each character.

1. 言
   a. yān   b. yēn   c. yīn   d. yán

2. 見
   a. jīng   b. jiàn   c. jiēn   d. jàng

3. 和
   a. hū   b. hé   c. hòu   d. hǒu

4. 星
   a. xìng   b. xīng   c. shēng   d. shuō

5. 爸
   a. běn   b. pù   c. bù   d. bà

6. 久
   a. jiǔ   b. tǔ   c. pēn   d. dàn

D. Identify the compound word or phrase that is related to each English concept.

1. movie star
   a. 學期　　b. 明星　　c. 星期　　d. 木星

2. thanks
   a. 謝謝　　b. 不謝　　c. 身家　　d. 過期

3. for a long time
   a. 見地　　b. 不見　　c. 久久　　d. 不久

4. spoken language
   a. 國文　　b. 文言　　c. 多言　　d. 口語

5. to meet with
   a. 會見　　b. 回來　　c. 出身　　d. 年會

6. week
   a. 星星　　b. 星期　　c. 孕期　　d. 多謝

E. Identify the compound word or phrase that is related to each pinyin transcription.

1. rìjiǔ
   a. 回見　　b. 日出　　c. 不久　　d. 日久

2. shēnyùn
   a. 語言　　b. 土語　　c. 身孕　　d. 下身

3. kànjian
   a. 看見　　b. 會見　　c. 見過　　d. 看出

4. héhǎo
   a. 和會　　b. 和好　　c. 太好　　d. 不和

5. bàba
   a. 謝謝　　b. 學校　　c. 爸爸　　d. 媽媽

6. qiànshēn
   a. 身上　　b. 本身　　c. 生前　　d. 前身

F. Identify the character that is different in tone from the others.

1.   a. 星   b. 久   c. 好   d. 本

2.   a. 那   b. 語   c. 地   d. 謝

3.   a. 期   b. 美   c. 本   d. 小

4.   a. 爸   b. 國   c. 和   d. 來

5.   a. 見   b. 媽   c. 謝   d. 下

6.   a. 言   b. 語   c. 前   d. 和

7.   a. 孕   b. 爸   c. 見   d. 久

8.   a. 身   b. 書   c. 出   d. 會

G. Fill in the blanks with the appropriate words or phrases.

1.   ——星期六我去看馬大夫。
     a. 下   b. 明   c. 昨   d. 去

2.   今天早上我 ——一個明星。
     a. 看看   b. 看見   c. 好看   d. 說過

3.   她去日本的——是五月二十五。
     a. 星期   b. 學期   c. 日期   d. 日前

4.   馬先生——馬太太都是上海人。
     a. 很   b. 每   c. 也   d. 和

5.   她——很多土語。
     a. 會說   b. 看了   c. 會看   d. 什麼

6.   牛子山——說國語。
     a. 很好   b. 不明   c. 不會   d. 不和

7.   —— 沒有看見她了。
     a. 很久   b. 星期   c. 是嗎   d. 不久

8.   我爸爸是一個語言 ——。
     a. 外人   b. 本人   c. 學家   d. 小家

H.   Rearrange the word groups to form meaningful sentences.

     1.   會說，你，會不，國語？

     2.   星星，天上，很多，有。

     3.   不在，我，家，星期天。

     4.   見，很，不，久。

     5.   出身，很好，人，這個。

     6.   語言，不好，學，中國。

     7.   和她，我，美國人，都是。

I.   Translate the following into English.

     1.   她下星期五來我家。

     2.   我今天早上看見她。

     3.   你會不會說日語？

     4.   謝謝你來看我。

     5.   爸爸和媽媽都是國文先生。

J. Translate the following into Chinese.

    1.   Is today Friday?

    2.   His mother has a younger sister and a younger brother.

    3.   My father can speak both Japanese and Mandarin.

    4.   My father is a linguist.

    5.   Mrs. Lin is four months pregnant.

Answers

A.	B.	C.	D.	E.
1. c	1. d	1. d	1. b	1. d
2. d	2. a	2. b	2. a	2. c
3. a	3. a	3. b	3. c	3. a
4. b	4. b	4. b	4. d	4. b
5. d	5. a	5. d	5. a	5. c
6. b	6. c	6. a	6. b	6. d
7. c	7. d			
8. d	8. c			
9. c				
10. c				

F.	G.	H.
1. a	1. a	1. 你會不會說國語？
2. b	2. b	2. 天上有很多星星。
3. a	3. c	3. 我星期天不在家。(星期天我不在家。)
4. a	4. d	4. 很久不見。
5. b	5. a	5. 這個人出身很好。
6. b	6. c	6. 中國語言不好學。
7. d	7. a	7. 我和她都是美國人。
8. d	8. c	

I.

1. She will come to my home next Friday.
2. I saw her this morning.
3. Do you speak Japanese?
4. Thank you for coming to see me.
5. My father and my mother are both teachers of the Chinese language.

J.

1. 今天是不是星期五？(今天是星期五嗎？)
2. 他媽媽有一個妹妹和一個弟弟。
3. 我爸爸會說日語和國語。
4. 我爸爸是一個語言學家。
5. 林太太有四個月的身孕。

第十課

Lesson 10

教

| | jiāo | teach; instruct | |
| | jiào | teach; instruct; religion | |

教書	jiāoshū	teach school	教书
教學	jiāoxué	teaching; instruction	教学
教本	jiàoběn	textbook	教本
教父	jiàofù	godfather	教父
教母	jiàomǔ	godmother	教母
教會	jiàohuì	church	教会
教友	jiàoyǒu	members of the church	教友
見教	jiànjiào	to instruct me	见教
回教	huíjiào	Islam	回教
家教	jiājiào	family education and discipline	家教
身教	shēnjiào	to teach by example	身教
教會學校	jiàohuìxuéxiào	a missionary school	教会学校

英

| | yīng | handsome; brave; heroic; English; a surname | |

英國	Yīngguó	England; Britain	英国
英明	yīngmíng	wise; brilliant	英明
英文	yīngwén	English language (written)	英文

英語	yīngyǔ	English language (spoken)	英语
英年	yīngnián	years of youthful vigor	英年
英美	yīngměi	Anglo-American	英美
英國人	yīngguórén	Englishman; British person	英国人

她爸爸在教會學校教書。
Her father teaches at a missionary school.

她爸爸在教会学校教书。
Tā bàba zài jiàohuì xuéxiào jiāoshū.

我們都是那教會的教友。
We are members of that church.

我们都是那教会的教友。
Wǒmen dōu shì nà jiàohuì de jiàoyǒu.

馬先生教中文教了三年了。
Mr. Ma has been teaching Chinese for three years.

马先生教中文教了三年了。
Mǎ xiānsheng jiāo zhōngwén jiāo le sān nián le.

她會說英語、日語、和國語。
She can speak English, Japanese, and Mandarin Chinese.

她会说英语、日语、和国语。
Tā huì shuō yīngyǔ, rìyǔ, hé guóyǔ.

教我們英文的先生是英國人。
The teacher who teaches us English is British.

教我们英文的先生是英国人。
Jiāo wǒmen yīngwén de xiānsheng shì Yīngguórén.

英先生教英國文學教了五年了。
Mr. Ying has taught English literature for five years.

英先生教英国文学教了五年了。
Yīng xiānsheng jiāo yīngguówénxué jiāo le wǔ nián le.

英先生教了五年的英國文學。
Mr. Ying has taught English literature for five years.

英先生教了五年的英国文学。
Yīng xiānsheng jiāo le wǔ nián de yīngguówénxué.

病 bìng illness; disease; fault

病夫	bìngfū	someone who is sick frequently	病夫
病人	bìngrén	patient	病人

病友	bìngyǒu	a fellow patient	病友
生病	shēngbìng	to be sick	生病
有病	yǒubìng	sick; ill	有病
心病	xīnbìng	secret grudge	心病
看病	kànbìng	see a doctor; see a patient	看病

現 现　　xiàn　　now; present; appear

現在	xiànzài	now; at present	現在
現今	xiànjīn	nowadays; these days	現今
現下	xiànxià	now; at present	現下
現有	xiànyǒu	existing	現有
現出	xiànchū	show	現出
出現	chūxiàn	appear; emerge	出現

英大夫有很多病人。
Dr. Ying has many patients.

英大夫有很多病人。
Yīng dàifu yǒu hěn duō bìngrén.

你是不是有病了。
Are you feeling sick?

你是不是有病了。
Nǐ shì bu shì yǒu bìng le?

我很好，我沒有病。
I am very fine. I am not sick.

我很好，我没有病。
Wǒ hěn hǎo, wǒ méi yǒu bìng.

你的病好了沒有？
Have you recovered from your illness?

你的病好了没有？
Nǐ de bìng hǎo le méiyou?

好了，謝謝你。
I am okay now, thank you.

好了，谢谢你。
Hǎo le, xièxie nǐ.

他病了多久？
How long has he been ill?

他病了多久？
Tā bìng le duō jiǔ?

139

他病了三個星期。
He has been ill for three weeks.

他病了三个星期。
Tā bìng le sānge xīngqī.

他病了三天，現在好了。
He was sick for three days. He is okay now.

他病了三天，现在好了。
Tā bìng le sān tiān, xiānzài hǎo le.

我現在什麼都沒有了。
I don't have anything left now.

我现在什么都没有了。
Wǒ xiànzài shénme dōu méi yǒu le.

她天天都在門口出現。
She shows up at the door every day.

她天天都在门口出现。
Tā tiāntiān dōu zài ménkǒu chūxiàn.

我們現在在什麼地方？
Where are we located at this moment?

我们现在在什么地方？
Wǒmen xiànzài zài shénme dìfang?

共 gòng together; common; share

共 生	gòngshēng	symbiosis	共 生
共 和	gònghé	a republic	共 和
共 有	gòngyǒu	owned by all	共 有
一 共	yígòng	altogether	一 共
中 共	zhōnggòng	the Communist Party of China	中 共

次 cì the next in order; secondary; inferior; a measure word

次 次	cìcì	every time	次 次
次 日	cìrì	the next day	次 日
次 女	cìnǔ	the second daughter	次 女
次 子	cìzǐ	the second son	次 子
每 次	měicì	each time; every time	每 次

上次	shàngcì	last time	上次
下次	xiàcì	next time	下次
一次	yícì	once	一次
有一次	yǒuyícì	on one occasion	有一次

我一共有五本中文書。
I have a total of five Chinese books.

我一共有五本中文书。
Wǒ yígòng yǒu wǔběn zhōngwén shū.

這是我們大家共有的。
This is owned by all of us.

这是我们大家共有的。
Zhè shì wǒmen dàjiā gòngyǒu de.

英先生和英太太一共有五個子女。
Mr. and Mrs. Ying have five children altogether.

英先生和英太太一共有五个子女。
Yīng xiānsheng hé Yīng tàitai yígòng yǒu wǔge zǐnǔ.

我下次會來看你。
I will come to see you next time.

我下次会来看你。
Wǒ xiàcì huì lái kàn nǐ.

我一共去過日本三次。
I have visited Japan three times altogether.

我一共去过日本三次。
Wǒ yígòng qùguo Rìběn sāncì.

有一次我在學校看見她。
I saw her on one occasion at school.

有一次我在学校看见她。
Yǒu yícì wǒ zài xuéxiào kànjian tā.

她來過很多次。
She came here many times.

她来过很多次。
Tā láiguo hěn duō cì.

我每次去他都不在。
Every time I went there he was not in.

我每次去他都不在。
Wǒ měicì qù tā dōu bú zài.

他一次也沒有去過上海。
He has never been to Shanghai.

他一次也没有去过上海。
Tā yícì yě méi yǒu qùguo Shànghǎi.

時 时　　shí　　time; hour; season

時 期	shíqī	period	时 期
時 時	shíshí	often; frequently	时 时
時 人	shírén	people from the same era	时 人
時 日	shírì	time and day	时 日
時 下	shíxià	nowadays	时 下
時 雨	shíyǔ	rain (which occurs at the right time)	时 雨
有 時	yǒushí	sometimes	有 时
小 時	xiǎoshí	hour	小 时
四 時	sìshí	the four seasons	四 时
天 時	tiānshí	weather; climate	天 时
多 時	duōshí	a long time	多 时
一 時	yìshí	accidentally; for a short while	一 时

候　　hòu　　wait; expect; season; time

候 教	hòujiào	awaiting instructions (polite expression)	候 教
時 候	shíhòu	a point in time; the duration of time	时 候
火 候	huǒhou	time required in cooking	火 候

我明天早上九時來你家。
I will come to your home at nine o'clock tomorrow morning.

天時不好，他回家去了。
The weather was bad, so he went home already.

我明天早上九时来你家。
Wǒ míngtiān zǎoshang jiǔ shí lái nǐ jiā.

天时不好，他回家去了。
Tiānshí bù hǎo, tā huí jiā le.

我昨天一共看了三小時的小説。
I spent a total of three hours reading a novel yesterday.

我昨天一共看了三小时的小说。
Wǒ zuótiān yígòng kàn le sān xiǎoshí de xiǎoshuō.

日子有時好過，有時不好過。
Life is sometimes easy and sometimes hard.

日子有时好过，有时不好过。
Rìzǐ yǒu shí hǎo guò, yǒu shí bù hǎo guò.

一天有二十四小時。
There are twenty-four hours in a day.

一天有二十四小时。
Yìtiān yǒu èrshísì xiǎoshí.

我們多時沒看見她了。
We haven't seen her for quite some time.

我们多时没看见她了。
Wǒmen duōshí méi kànjian tā le.

現在是什麼時候了？
What time is it now?

现在是什么时候了？
Xiànzài shì shénme shíhou le?

你什麼時候去學校？
When will you go to school?

你什么时候去学校？
Nǐ shénme shíhou qù xuéxiào?

我晚上在家候教。
I will be home tonight awaiting your instructions.

我晚上在家候教。
Wǒ wǎnshang zài jiā hòujiào.

高	gāo	high; tall; height; a surname	
高大	gāodà	tall and big	高大
高地	gāodì	high ground	高地
高中	gāozhōng	senior high school	高中
高見	gāojiàn	wise opinion	高见
高明	gāomíng	wise; clever	高明
高年	gāonián	advanced in age	高年
高人	gāorén	tall man	高人
高下	gāoxià	up and down; relative height or value	高下

高山	gāoshān	high mountain	高山
高個子	gāogèzi	tall person	高个子
高高在上	gāogāo -zàishàng	stand high above the others	高高在上

城　　　　　chéng　　　wall; city; town

城外　　　chéngwài　　outside of town　　　　　城外

高先生是個高個子。
Mr. Gao is a tall man.

你有什麼高見？
Do you have any opinion?

中國有很多高山和大川。
There are many high mountains and
big rivers in China.

高小姐很高，她也很好看。
Miss Gao is very tall, and she is also very
attractive.

我沒有他那麼高明。
I am not as wise as he.

我弟弟今年高了很多。
My younger brother has grown much taller
this year.

上海是一個人口很多的大城。
Shanghai is a big city with a huge population.

高先生是个高个子。
Gāo xiānsheng shì ge gāogèzi.

你有什么高见？
Nǐ yǒu shénme gāojiàn?

中国有很多高山和大川。
Zhōngguó yǒu hěn duō gāo shān hé dà
chuān.

高小姐很高，她也很好看。
Gāo Xiéojie hěn gāo, tā yě hěn hǎo kàn.

我没有他那么高明。
Wǒ méiyǒu tā nàme gāomíng.

我弟弟今年高了很多。
Wǒ dìdi jīnnián gāo le hěn duō.

上海是一个人口很多的大城。
Shànghǎi shì yíge rénkǒu hěn duō de dà
chéng.

144

我 的 出 生 地 是 一 個 小 城 。
My birthplace is a small town.

我 的 出 生 地 是 一 个 小 城 。
Wǒ de chūshēngdì shì yíge xiǎo chéng.

他 們 的 家 都 是 在 城 外 。
Their homes are all in the suburbs.

他 们 的 家 都 是 在 城 外 。
Tāmen de jiā dōu shì zài chéngwài.

同		tóng	same; common; agree; together		
同	好	tónghào	people with the same hobby	同	好
同	年	tóngnián	same age	同	年
同	時	tóngshí	same time	同	时
同	期	tóngqī	same period of time	同	期
同	上	tóngshàng	ditto; something previously mentioned	同	上
同	學	tóngxué	schoolmate	同	学
同	心	tóngxīn	like-minded	同	心
同	日	tóngrì	same day	同	日
同	一	tóngyī	same; identical	同	一
一	同	yìtóng	together	一	同
不	同	bùtóng	different	不	同
共	同	gòngtóng	common	共	同

只		zhǐ	only; merely; but yet		
只	好	zhǐhǎo	be forced to	只	好
只	會	zhǐhuì	only know how to	只	会
只	是	zhǐshì	only; however	只	是
只	有	zhǐyǒu	only; alone	只	有
不	只	bùzhǐ	not only; more than	不	只
只	不 過	zhǐbúguò	only; just; merely	只	不 过

中國有很多不同的方言。
There are many different dialects in China.

中国有很多不同的方言。
Zhōngguó yǒu hěn duō bùtóng de fāngyán.

我們有一個共同的目的。
We have a common purpose.

我们有一个共同的目的。
Wǒmen yǒu yíge gòngtóng de mùdì.

他們是同年同月同日生的。
They were born the same day, same month, and same year.

他们是同年同月同日生的。
Tāmen shì tóngnián, tóngyuè, tóngrì shēng de.

我們明天一同去上海。
We are going to Shanghai together tomorrow.

我们明天一同去上海。
Wǒmen míngtiān yìtóng qù Shànghǎi.

她有病，我只好一個人去。
She was sick, so I was forced to go alone.

她有病，我只好一个人去。
Tā yǒu bìng, wǒ zhǐhǎo yíge rén qù.

她很好看，只是心地不好。
She is attractive, but she has an evil mind.

她很好看，只是心地不好。
Tā hěn hǎokàn, zhǐshì xīndì bù hǎo.

我去過中國不只一次。
I went to China more than once.

我去过中国不只一次。
Wǒ qùquo Zhōngquó bùzhǐ yícì.

我只不過學了一年中文。
I have been studying the Chinese language for just a year.

我只不过学了一年中文。
Wǒ zhǐbúguò xué le yìnián Zhōngwén.

我只有一本日文書。
I have only one Japanese language book.

我 只有一本日文书。
Wǒ zhǐyǒu yìběn rìwén shū.

在我們同學中，只有她會説土語。
Among our classmates, only she can speak the dialect.

在我们同学中，只有她会说土语。
Zài wǒmen tóngxué zhōng, zhǐyǒu tā huì shuō tǔyǔ.

我們一同去，好不好？
How about let's go together?

我们一同去，好不好？
Wǒmen yìtóng qù, hǎo bu hǎo?

Exercises Lesson 10

A. Identify the character that is related to each English word or phrase.

1. brave
   a. 方　　　b. 英　　　c. 星　　　d. 和

2. to teach
   a. 回　　　b. 多　　　c. 教　　　d. 學

3. illness
   a. 病　　　b. 內　　　c. 河　　　d. 開

4. tall
   a. 念　　　b. 等　　　c. 高　　　d. 里

5. same
   a. 凡　　　b. 平　　　c. 年　　　d. 同

6. city
   a. 地　　　b. 城　　　c. 位　　　d. 或

7. hour
   a. 相　　　b. 亮　　　c. 時　　　d. 光

8. together
   a. 共　　　b. 工　　　c. 交　　　d. 可

9. secondary
   a. 也　　　b. 久　　　c. 化　　　d. 次

10. now
    a. 每　　　b. 現　　　c. 先　　　d. 昨

B. Identify the character that is related to each pinyin transcription.

1. xiàn
   a. 什　　　b. 身　　　c. 現　　　d. 生

2. chéng
   a. 城   b. 和   c. 候   d. 前

3. shí
   a. 會   b. 期   c. 是   d. 時

4. zhǐ
   a. 星   b. 只   c. 十   d. 這

5. tóng
   a. 同   b. 中   c. 看   d. 共

6. gāo
   a. 晶   b. 尖   c. 亮   d. 高

7. jiào
   a. 候   b. 病   c. 教   d. 家

8. yīng
   a. 次   b. 英   c. 年   d. 現

C. Identify the pinyin transcription that is related to each character.

1. 病
   a. bàng   b. bēng   c. bìng   d. pēng

2. 共
   a. jìng   b. gēng   c. guàng   d. gòng

3. 候
   a. hū   b. háu   c. hòu   d. hé

4. 時
   a. shēn   b. shì   c. shí   d. shū

5. 高
   a. gāo   b. gàng   c. gè   d. gǎo

6. 現
   a. xiàn   b. xīn   c. sàn   d. xià

D. Identify the compound word or phrase that is related to each English word or phrase.

1. church
    a. 教學   b. 身教   c. 教本   d. 教會

2. now
    a. 現在   b. 出現   c. 現出   d. 現有

3. to see a doctor
    a. 病夫   b. 生病   c. 有病   d. 看病

4. altogether
    a. 共生   b. 一共   c. 中共   d. 共和

5. at times
    a. 時人   b. 是日   c. 有時   d. 小時

6. a point in time
    a. 時候   b. 火候   c. 星期   d. 時下

E. Identify the compound word or phrase that is related to each pinyin transcription.

1. xiǎoshí
    a. 教書   b. 四時   c. 小説   d. 小時

2. tóngxué
    a. 同學   b. 同期   c. 同上   d. 同時

3. zhǐhuì
    a. 回教   b. 只好   c. 只是   d. 只會

4. yīngměi
    a. 英語   b. 也門   c. 英明   d. 英美

5. gāojiàn
    a. 高見   b. 高中   c. 高年   d. 高下

6. bìngyǒu
    a. 病人   b. 有病   c. 病友   d. 病夫

F.   Identify the character that is different in tone from the others.

1.   a. 語   b. 高   c. 方   d. 山

2.   a. 前   b. 城   c. 人   d. 只

3.   a. 同   b. 國   c. 昨   d. 病

4.   a. 共   b. 在   c. 英   d. 現

5.   a. 教   b. 次   c. 書   d. 會

6.   a. 候   b. 言   c. 時   d. 城

7.   a. 只   b. 久   c. 小   d. 謝

6.   a. 英   b. 說   c. 時   d. 出

G.   Fill in the blanks with the appropriate words or phrases.

1.   她的病——沒有？
     a. 不好   b. 好了   c. 生出   d. 過去

2.   他學英文——很久。
     a. 學了   b. 會說   c. 三年   d. 不會

3.   現在是——八時。
     a. 時期   b. 晚上   c. 很早   d. 只有

4.   我——去過英國五次。
     a. 共同   b. 有時   c. 同時   d. 一共

5.   英語和日語有很多——的地方。
     a. 好看   b. 不同   c. 不只   d. 和好

6.   我——三本英文小說。
     a. 不會   b. 會說   c. 只會   d. 只有

7. 你明天──時候來？
   a. 早上　　b. 什麼　　c. 共有　　d. 一同

8. 中山小學是在──。
   a. 城外　　b. 家中　　c. 上學　　d. 中外

H. Rearrange the word groups to form meaningful sentences.

1. 英語，教了，她，三年的 。

2. 是，生的，什麼病，她 ？

3. 現在，你，去，哪兒 ？

4. 一次，我，英國，去過 。

5. 同學，只是，我的，她 。

6. 一共，十個人，有，同學會 。

7. 教書，五年，他，教了 。

I. Translate the following into English.

1. 你每天什麼時候上學？

2. 你是不是生病了？

3. 你們是同學嗎？

4. 英先生教高中學生。

5. 她一共去過英國三次。

J. Translate the following into Chinese.

    1.   What time is it now?

    2.   He went to Japan three times the year before last year.

    3.   What do you teach?

    4.   I have only one younger brother.

    5.   That foreigner is very tall.

Answers

A.	B.	C.	D.	E.
1. b	1. c	1. c	1. d	1. d
2. c	2. a	2. d	2. a	2. a
3. a	3. d	3. c	3. d	3. d
4. c	4. b	4. c	4. b	4. d
5. d	5. a	5. a	5. c	5. a
6. b	6. d	6. a	6. a	6. c
7. c	7. c			
8. a	8. b			
9. d				
10. b				

F.	G.	H.
1. a	1. b	1. 她教了三年的英語。
2. d	2. a	2. 她生的是什麼病？
3. d	3. b	3. 你現在去哪兒？
4. c	4. d	4. 我去過英國一次。
5. c	5. b	5. 她只是我的同學。
6. a	6. d	6. 同學會一共有十個人。
7. d	7. b	7. 他教書教了五年。
8. c	8. a	

I

1. What time do you go to school every day?
2. Are you sick?
3. Are you schoolmates?
4. Mr. Ying teaches senior high school students.
5. She went to England three times altogether.

J.

1. 現在是什麼時候？
2. 他前年去過日本三次。
3. 你教的是什麼？
4. 我只有一個弟弟。
5. 那外國人很高。

Chinese Index

English Index

M

N

O

Easy Chinese Tutor CD-ROM

Agreement

By using the accompanying *Easy Chinese Tutor* CD-ROM, you are agreeing to be bound by the following:

This CD-ROM (*Easy Chinese Tutor*) may only be used by the original purchaser on a single computer. No part of this software program may be reproduced or transmitted in any form or by any means, including copying, recording, or duplicating, without prior written permission of the publisher. The author and Emnes Systems assume no liability for any errors or inaccuracies that may appear on this CD-ROM or in the accompanying manual.

This CD-ROM is sold as is, with no warranty of any kind, expressed or implied. In the event that the software fails to run on a target computer due to manufacturing defects, the maximum amount to be refunded shall not exceed the purchase price. Neither the publisher nor the author assumes any liability for any alleged or actual damages caused by the use of this software program.

How do I start the *Easy Chinese Tutor* CD- ROM?

- Insert the *Easy Chinese Tutor* CD-ROM into the CD-ROM drive.
- Click the start button and select **Run**.
- Type E:\ezch1\chn.exe and press Enter.
  (Make appropriate substitution if E is not the letter that corresponds to your CD-ROM drive.)

For additional information on how to use the program, please refer to the "Frequently Asked Questions" section of the manual.